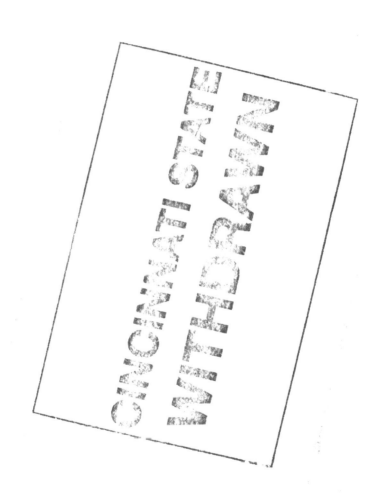

Kenneth E. Clow, PhD
Donald Baack, PhD

Concise Encyclopedia of Advertising

*Pre-publication
REVIEWS,
COMMENTARIES,
EVALUATIONS . . .*

"**A** valuable reference for academic and public libraries alike, the *Concise Encyclopedia of Advertising* is also a wonderful resource for students, faculty, and businesspeople as well as those working professionally in the marketing and advertising fields. The alphabetical ordering of terms and phrases makes finding information a breeze, while the descriptions provide users with an easy-to-read definition and much more in the way of valuable information! The additional facts, trends, and other pertinent information included under each term enhance the overall value of the publication, while the reader-friendly writing style ensures that those with limited marketing or advertising knowledge can easily grasp the essence of each concept. Furthermore, many entries contain cross-references to related terms, ensuring that those wishing to learn more can easily find and read additional information. Whether you're a businessperson who must deal with one or more members of the advertising industry, a faculty member or professional in the marketing or advertising industry, or a college student studying advertising, public relations, or marketing, Clow and Baack's *Concise Encyclopedia of Advertising* is an exceptional resource that deserves a place on your bookshelf."

Karen E. James, DBA
*Associate Professor,
Louisiana State University–Shreveport*

"**T**he *Concise Encyclopedia of Advertising* is a valuable resource for academicians, students, and professionals alike. It provides a wealth of information from industry terminology to job descriptions to scholarly definitions. Even the most complex advertising concepts are explained in a succinct, easy-to-understand manner. As a result, it is the perfect addition to the library of anyone working in or interested in advertising."

Kristine Kranenburg, MS
*Assistant Professor,
School of Journalism,
Southern Illinois University–Carbondale*

Best Business Books®
The Haworth Reference Press™
Imprints of The Haworth Press, Inc.
New York • London • Oxford

Concise Encyclopedia
of Advertising

BEST BUSINESS BOOKS®
Robert E. Stevens, PhD
David L. Loudon, PhD
Editors in Chief

Concise Encyclopedia
of Advertising

Kenneth E. Clow, PhD
Donald Baack, PhD

Best Business Books®
The Haworth Reference Press™
Imprints of The Haworth Press, Inc.
New York • London • Oxford

For more information on this book or to order, visit
http://www.haworthpress.com/store/product.asp?sku=5295

or call 1-800-HAWORTH (800-429-6784) in the United States
and Canada or (607) 722-5857 outside the United States and Canada

or contact orders@HaworthPress.com

Published by

Best Business Books® and The Haworth Reference Press™, imprints of The Haworth Press, Inc.,
10 Alice Street, Binghamton, NY 13904-1580.

Cover design by Jennifer M. Gaska.

Library of Congress Cataloging-in-Publication Data

Clow, Kenneth, E.
    Concise encyclopedia of advertising / Kenneth E. Clow, Donald Baack.
       p. cm.'
    Includes bibliographical references and index.
    ISBN 0-7890-2210-9 (hard : alk. paper) — ISBN 0-7890-2211-7 (soft : alk. paper)
    1. Advertising—Encyclopedias. I. Baack, Donald. II. Title.

HF5803.C59 2005
659.1'03—dc22

                                     2004013359

CONTENTS

ABOUT THE AUTHORS

Kenneth E. Clow, PhD, is the Dean of the College of Business Administration at the University of Louisiana at Monroe. He previously served as the Dean for the University of North Carolina at Pembroke and as the MBA Director at Pittsburg State University. He has published over 120 articles in academic journals and proceedings. Dr. Clow has written numerous articles in the area of advertising and has spoken at a number of public events on various advertising topics. His advertising research has focused on the impact of visual elements of print ads and their role in advertising.

Donald Baack, PhD, is a professor in the Department of Management and Marketing at Pittsburg State University. He has participated in numerous marketing and advertising conferences, including the Society for Marketing Advances, American Marketing Association, and the American Academy of Advertising, among others. He co-authored two papers that received Best Paper awards at the Southwest Decision Sciences meeting and at the Southwest Academy of Management conference. Dr. Baack has also co-authored a textbook with Kenneth Clow and has prepared three popular press books in the areas of self-help and romance.

Preface

Every day, consumers are surrounded by advertising in all forms, from the television shows they watch to the magazines they read to the billboards they see while traveling. Advertising is a pervasive institution in the United States as well as throughout the world. As with many institutions, advertising has developed its own unique vocabulary. Although some of the terms and concepts used in advertising overlap with other subjects, such as marketing, many are used in a particular way and have specific meanings to advertisers.

This *Concise Encyclopedia of Advertising* was written to provide marketers, advertisers, consumers, and businesses with a quick reference to the terminology used in the advertising industry. These brief definitions and explanations provide information about the basic advertising concepts. This guide will allow you to understand and utilize these terms from the fields of advertising and marketing.

ABILITY TO SEARCH

The ability to search plays a role in the consumer purchase decision process, as part of the search for information. In the first step of a consumer purchase decision a consumer has recognized a need or desire. Next, the individual searches his or her memory for information about how the need or desire has been met in the past. If enough information is available internally, the consumer proceeds to make a decision. If the decision concerns a high-involvement purchase or one that the person has little knowledge about, the consumer goes beyond memories and conducts an external search for additional information. The extent or level of this external search is partly determined by the consumer's ability to search.

A person's educational level combined with specific knowledge of the product category and the brands being offered contribute to the individual's ability to search. Educational levels and tendencies to conduct external searches are closely related. Consumers who are more educated are more likely to search for product information. Many will visit stores prior to making a decision. Also, consumers with extensive knowledge about individual brands and product categories are able to conduct more extensive external searches. A person with a more comprehensive knowledge of a product area often collects additional information even when he or she is not in the market for the product.[1]

ACCELERATION PRINCIPLE

When the demand for a consumer product increases, it normally sparks the demand for new equipment and new buildings as companies expand to handle increased production.[2] Thus, a small increase in consumer demand of 10 to 15 percent can cause as much as a 200 percent increase in the demand for machines, equipment, and supplies needed to meet the demand. This acceleration occurs not only during times when demand expands but also as demand contracts. Consequently, a seemingly small 10 percent decrease in consumer demand can cause a complete collapse in business demand for machines and equipment used to manufacture that product. Thus, small changes in consumer demand usually have much larger impacts on demand for business goods and services that are used in the production process because of its derived nature.

ACCOUNT EXECUTIVE

An account executive is a person who is employed by an advertising agency or similar type of marketing firm. The role of the account executive is to solicit new clients and to work on behalf of clients. The account executive meets with a client to discuss the client's marketing and advertising needs. Those needs determine the activities of the advertising agency's creatives and others working on the account. There is, or should be, continual communication between the agency and the client as an advertising campaign is developed. The account executive serves as the liaison, or go-between, representing the interests of both the client and the agency.

Account executives are experiencing an increasing demand for accountability by clients. They are under pressure to produce tangible results from advertising efforts. The executive is carefully scrutinized by the client firm. As a result, many account executives work directly with clients to develop an integrated marketing plan as well as strategic plans. The goal is to ensure that the advertising work of the agency fits into the client's strategic marketing plans and will yield successful results.

ACTION-INDUCING CONATIVE MESSAGE STRATEGY

A message strategy is the primary tactic used by a creative to deliver the message theme. Message strategies can be divided into four types: cognitive, affective, conative, and brand. Action-inducing message strategies are a subgroup of conative message strategies. Cona-

tive message strategies are related to the conative component of attitude. They are used in advertisements that encourage some type of
action or behavior on the part of the person who encounters the message.

An advertisement using an action-inducing type of conative message strategy attempts to persuade consumers or businesses to act or
behave in some particular manner. Actions include making a purchase, making telephone calls, accessing Web sites, and requesting
additional information. Action-inducing message strategies are based
on situations in which cognitive knowledge of a product or affective
liking of a product may come later, after the actual purchase or during
the use of the product. Action is often linked to items such as impulse
buys. In that situation, the idea is to make the sale, with affective feelings and cognitive knowledge forming about the product after or during the time the product is consumed.

ADAPTATION

Adaptation is a marketing strategy used by firms seeking to expand
sales to other countries. Adaptation occurs when a company's products and marketing messages are redesigned or adapted to fit individual countries. Thus, the advertising or marketing message that is used
in France would be different than that used in Germany, Brazil, Canada, the United States, or any other country in which the company operates. In addition to adapting the marketing message to fit each nation, the product may also be modified to fit the tastes and interests of
the region. The ingredients in many soft drinks are altered to match
consumer tastes in each individual country.

ADMINISTRATIVE COMPLAINT

An administrative complaint is part of the process of ensuring that
advertisements are truthful and do not intentionally mislead consumers. A false or misleading advertisement may result in a complaint being filed with the Federal Trade Commission (FTC), which begins an
official investigation. If the FTC concludes that a violation has oc-

curred, it issues a consent order whereby the company or advertising agency agrees to discontinue the practice or advertisement without any admission of guilt.

If a consent agreement cannot be reached, the FTC then issues an administrative complaint. A formal proceeding similar to a court trial is then held before an administrative law judge. Both sides are permitted to submit evidence and render testimony. If the judge concludes that a violation has not occurred, the case is dismissed. If the judge concludes there was a violation, a cease and desist order will be rendered. The cease and desist order requires the company to stop the disputed practice or advertisement immediately and to refrain from similar future actions.

ADVERTISING AGENCY SELECTION

One of the key functions of advertising is selecting an advertising agency. The first decision is whether to use an external agency or in-house department. In making this decision, several major items are assessed.[3]

The first issue studied is the size of the account. A small account is not usually attractive to an advertising agency because small accounts generate lower revenues. Smaller accounts are also less economically sound for the agency, because more money must be spent on production of advertisements rather than purchasing media time or space. Agencies often utilize what is called the 75/15/10 breakdown. That is, 75 percent of the money should be used to buy media time or space, 15 percent should go to the agency for the creative work, and 10 percent should be spent on the actual production of the ad. For smaller accounts, the breakdown may be 25/40/35, meaning only 25 percent of the funds are spent on media purchases, and 75 percent goes to the creative and production work. Unless 75 percent of the company's advertising budget can be spent on media purchases, it may be wise either to do the work in-house or to develop contracts with smaller, specialty firms to prepare various aspects of the advertising campaign.

Another factor is objectivity. An agency is likely to be more objective than an in-house advertising department. Creatives working in-house are members of the company instead of an independent ad agency. It may be difficult for in-house creatives to remain unbiased and to ignore the influence of others in the organization who may not fully understand the artistic aspects of advertising. There is one exception: advertisements for highly complex products. Agency members may have a difficult time understanding more complicated products. For complex products, in-house departments may work best. For generic or more standard and simple products, ad agencies offer greater advantages.

The final issue to consider in choosing an agency versus performing the work in-house is creativity. Most agencies claim they have greater creativity than any in-house department. The question to be answered is how well the company's creatives or freelancers can perform as compared to an agency's creatives.

ADVERTISING APPEAL

In an advertisement, the appeal is the general tone and nature of the commercial or message. One of seven major types of appeals is most likely to be utilized. The primary appeals are

- fear,
- humor,
- sex,
- music,
- rationality,
- emotions, and
- scarcity.

The appeal is chosen after a review of a creative brief and the objective of the advertisement. A means-ends chain can guide the creative in the selection of an appeal. The final choice will be based on the product being sold, the personal preferences of the advertising creative and the account executive, and the wishes of the client. In determining the type of appeal to use, advertisers consider both what would be appropriate and what might be inappropriate. For example, common wisdom has been that humor is inappropriate for some personal items and following tragedies, but is highly appropriate when the goal is to attract interest and attention. Sex appeals are not as effective for goods and services that are not related to sex. (*See* CREATIVE BRIEF; MEANS-ENDS THE-ORY; *and each type of appeal for additional information.*)

ADVERTISING CAMPAIGN MANAGEMENT

Managing an advertising campaign includes preparing and integrating a specific advertising program in conjunction with an overall integrated marketing communications theme. Typical advertising programs follow five steps:

1. Review the communications market analysis.
2. Establish communication objectives.
3. Review the communications budget.
4. Select the media in conjunction with the advertising agency.
5. Review the information with the advertising creative in the creative brief.

The advertising program should be consistent with previous activities performed as part of the larger integrated marketing communications program. The goal is to develop clear messages aimed at key target markets. Assessments of communications objectives and budgets provide necessary constraints. Media are chosen to logically integrate messages, normally with one primary medium and a series of secondary or support media. This information is finalized when the creative brief is prepared. (*See* CREATIVE BRIEF *for additional information.*)

AFFECT REFERRAL

One model used to portray the ways consumers evaluate purchase alternatives is known as affect referral. Affect referral suggests that a consumer chooses the brand that he or she likes best. The individual does not evaluate other brands and often does not even think about which attributes are important. Instead, the consumer simply makes repeat purchases of preferred brands. Soft drinks, toothpaste, chewing gum, and other convenience goods are normally purchased using this method. These purchases are made with low levels of involvement and are made frequently.

Consumers may quickly eliminate alternatives in the method suggested by the affect referral model for two reasons. First, they save mental energy. A quick choice is easier than going through the mental process of evaluating all of the possible alternatives. Some purchases basically do not deserve much effort.

Second, a person may have already spent a great deal of time examining product attributes, deciding which attributes were most critical, and reaching a decision about which product to buy. Going through the process again would be reinventing the wheel. After making the purchase, many consumers continue purchasing the same brand as long as the experience remains positive. (*See* EVOKED SET *and* MULTIATTRIBUTE APPROACH *for additional methods of evaluating purchase alternatives.*)

AFFECTIVE (COMPONENT OF ATTITUDE)

Attitude is a mental position taken toward a topic, person, event, object, company, or product. Attitudes influence a person's feelings, perceptions, learning processes, and subsequent behaviors. They consist of three components: affective, cognitive, and conative.

The affective component of attitude is the general feeling or emotion a person attaches to an object, person, idea, or, in the case of marketing, a product. People develop emotions or feelings toward specific brands as well as to product categories.

Some emotions or attitudes are relatively benign while others are strongly held. A product such as a pair of socks or a ballpoint pen may not evoke much of a feeling. Other products, including cigarettes, alcohol, swimsuits, condoms, or automobiles normally elicit much stronger feelings.

In advertising, one primary goal is to elicit emotional reactions to ads that translate into corresponding positive feelings toward the brand. A company may use celebrities or well-known athletes as advertising spokespersons in the hope that consumers will transfer liking for the person to the brand, thus inspiring additional purchases.

AFFECTIVE MESSAGE STRATEGY

A message strategy is the primary tactic used in the creation of an advertising message. Message strategies can be divided into four categories: cognitive, affective, conative, and brand. Affective message strategies are designed to invoke feelings and emotions and match those feelings with a good, service, or company. The technique, which is used in the development of advertisements, seeks to influence the affective component of attitude. The goal is to enhance the likability of the product, recall of the appeal, or comprehension of the advertisement. Affective strategies elicit emotions, which in turn affect the consumer's reasoning process, and finally lead to action. In other words, an emotion such as love may help convince a consumer that a safer but more expensive car is worth the money. Affective strategies fall into two categories: resonance and emotional. (*For more information about these two types of affective message strategies, see* EMOTIONAL MESSAGE STRATEGY *and* RESONANCE MESSAGE STRATEGY.)

AIDED RECALL

In evaluating an advertisement, aided recall is a testing method in which consumers are prompted with a product category and, if necessary, names of specific brands in that category. The subject does not know which brand or ad is being tested. When the consumer recalls seeing a specific brand being advertised, the person is then asked to provide as many details as possible about the ad. At that point, no further clues are given regarding the content of the ad. Recalling the advertisement increases the likelihood that the product will be purchased since the message and product have become part of the consumer's evoked set. (*See* EVOKED SET *for additional information.*)

ALTERNATIVE MEDIA

The traditional advertising media are television, radio, magazines, newspapers, billboards, and, more recently, the Internet. In addition, there are alternative media that companies can use to deliver advertising messages. The most important factor in selecting both traditional and alternative media is making certain the ads reach the right target market with the proper message. Examples of alternative forms of advertising, some of which are new and some of which have existed for many years, include the following:

- Leaflets, brochures, and carry-home menus
- Ads on carry-home bags from stores (grocery stores and retail outlets)
- Ads on T-shirts and caps (promotional giveaways and products sold)
- Ads on movie trailers both in theaters and on home video rental products
- Small, freestanding road signs
- Self-run ads in motel rooms on television, ashtrays, towels, ice chests, an so on.
- Yellow Pages and phone book advertisements
- Mall kiosk ads
- Ads sent by fax
- Ads shown on video replay scoreboards at major sports events
- In-house advertising magazines placed by airlines in seats
- Ads on the walls of airports, subway terminals, bus terminals, and inside cabs and buses

Each of these forms has benefits and problems. Small, freestanding road signs are quite effective at gaining attention, but are considered eyesores by many local governments and community citizens. Yellow Pages advertising has become more expensive as additional firms enter the phone book preparation market. Mall kiosk ads placed in high traffic areas are easily defaced by vandals. Ads sent by fax are low cost and can be highly targeted (for example, luncheon specials faxed to local companies just before noon). Still, many business owners become angry when their fax machines become tied up receiving ads.

Ads on replay scoreboards have high intrusion values, yet can be ignored or even booed by those attending the game. Nonetheless, advertisers must consider all of the possibilities as they prepare advertising campaigns. The goals of reach, frequency, continuity, and costs must all be considered as individual media are selected and media groups are incorporated into an advertisting campaign.

ANIMATION EXECUTION

Animation is a type of executional framework. Other types of executional frameworks include slice-of-life, dramatization, testimonials, authoritative, demonstration, fantasy, and informative. Many advertisers now use animation because of the greater sophistication in computer graphics programs. The technology now available to advertising creatives is far superior to the cartoon type that was previously used. For instance, the rotoscoping technique makes it possible to place hand-drawn characters digitally into live sequences. As a result, it is possible to present both live actors and animated characters in the same frame. Well-known live action television spots featuring cell animation included Michael Jordan and Bugs Bunny (and other cartoon characters) in MCI commercials. Animated characters can be human, animal, or product personifications.

Besides cartoons, another method of animation, which was made popular by the California Raisins commercials, is clay animation. Although expensive to create, clay animation has been successful. Another popular product personification is the Pillsbury Doughboy. Computer graphics technology now allows production companies to superimpose these animated personifications in live scenes.

Computer graphics technology has allowed animation to move beyond personifications into creating real-life images. This makes it possible to portray animals in settings where they would not otherwise be found. Animation is mostly used in television spots, though it can also be produced for movie trailers and Internet ads. Single shots of animated characters can be placed into print ads. Animation was a rarity in business-to-business advertising primarily because of the negative view most advertising agencies had of it, since many firms believed animation was appealing to children but was not for businesspeople. These conclusions have changed. More business ads are being placed on television because of the availability of high-quality graphics technologies that allow various businesses to illustrate the uses of their products through animated graphics.

APPEAL (ADVERTISING)

See ADVERTISING APPEAL.

ATTITUDE

Attitude is a mental position taken toward a topic, person, event, object, company, or product that influences a person's feelings, perceptions, learning processes, and subsequent behaviors. From an advertising perspective, attitudes drive actions. If a consumer has a positive attitude toward a brand, the propensity to actually purchase that brand is greater. If a person has a positive attitude toward a particular advertisement, it is likely the person will also have a positive attitude toward the brand and thus will be more inclined to buy.

Attitude consists of three components: (1) affective, (2) cognitive, and (3) conative. The affective component of attitude is the feelings and emotions a person attaches to a product, brand, or company. The cognitive component of attitude is the beliefs a person has about a product, brand, or company. The conative component of attitude is the action or behavioral side of attitude. The conative component includes consumer actions such as inquiring for additional information or making a purchase.

ATTITUDE OR OPINION TEST

Many of the tests used to evaluate advertisements are designed to examine attitudinal components. Attitude tests are often used in conjunction with recall or recognition tests. Attitude tests examine cognitive and affective reactions to an ad. They are normally designed to solicit consumer opinions about a marketing message. Opinions can be gathered from surveys or focus groups; they can also be obtained as part of a mall intercept plan or even in laboratory settings.

The content and format of attitude tests vary widely. Sometimes specific responses are requested in what are called closed-end questionnaire formats. Scales such as *1 = highly unfavorable* to *7 = highly favorable* are often prepared for respondents to answer. In other tests, the individual is allowed to discuss whatever comes to mind regarding some aspect of a product or its advertisements. These are called open-ended questions.

ATTRIBUTE POSITIONING

Positioning is the process of creating a perception in the minds of consumers concerning the nature of a brand relative to the competition. Possible positioning approaches include attributes, competitors, use or application, price-quality, product user, product class, and cultural symbols.

Attribute positioning is based on a product trait or characteristic that sets the brand apart from other products. A toothpaste may be positioned as the best product for preventing cavities because of unique ingredients. Milk can be positioned as the best source for calcium, which is needed for healthy bones in children as well as adults. The attribute positioning strategy is popular with advertisers because it allows the advertiser to focus on a particular attribute, characteristic, or benefit of the product being promoted.

AUTHORITATIVE EXECUTION

Authoritative execution is a type of executional framework. Other types of executional frameworks include animation, slice-of-life, dramatization, testimonials, demonstration, fantasy, and informative. In using the authoritative executional framework, the goal is to give the impression that a given product is superior to other brands, because of an authoritative source. One such source is an expert authority, such as a physician, dentist, engineer, or chemist stating the product's advantages over other brands. Less recognized experts such as automobile mechanics, professional house painters, nurses, or even aerobics instructors can also serve as authoritative spokespersons. These experts are used to explain the attributes of the brand that make the product superior.

Many authoritative advertisements include some type of scientific or survey evidence. Independent organizations, such as the American Medical Association, undertake a variety of product studies. Quoting the results gives an ad greater credibility. Survey results are less credible. Stating that four out of five dentists recommend a particular toothbrush or toothpaste is less effective, because the statement is too vague. When the American Medical Association states that an aspirin per day will reduce the risk of a second heart attack, however, the endorsement is highly credible. An aspirin company can take advantage of the finding by including it in their ads. The same is true when a magazine such as *Consumer Reports* ranks a particular brand as the best. Any scientific and independent source not paid by the advertising company makes an advertising claim more believable.

Authoritative ads work especially well in specialty magazines, because readers have an interest in the subject and are more likely to take time to process the information in the ad. In a hunting magazine, the use of an expert hunter is effective. Brides observe the endorsements of wedding experts in special bridal magazines. Readers notice specialized advertisements and the claims made have greater credibility. The same is true in business-to-business magazines. Trade journals are similar to specialty magazines in the business world. Authoritative advertisements have been widely incorporated into business-to-business sector ads, especially when scientific findings are available to provide support for a company's products.

BEHAVIORAL EVALUATION OF ADVERTISEMENTS

Behavioral evaluation of advertisements requires measuring some aspect of customer behavior, such as sales, inquiries, volume of store traffic, or the number of coupons redeemed. Many believe that the only valid evaluation criterion that should be used to evaluate any aspect of marketing, including advertising, is actual sales. To these critics, it is less important for an ad to be well liked. If an ad does not increase sales, then it is not effective. Measuring changes in sales following an advertising campaign is relatively easy today. Universal product codes and scanner data are available from many retail outlets. These data are available on a daily, weekly, or even real-time basis.

Scanner data make it possible for companies to monitor sales and help both the retailer and the manufacturer discover the impact of a particular advertising program. Bear in mind, however, that many factors can affect sales. For instance, in a multimedia advertising program, it would be difficult to know which ad moved the customer to action. Furthermore, a company may feature its fall line of jackets, and a cold snap may affect the region. If so, which caused the customer to buy the product, the ad or the weather? Firms utilizing trade and consumer promotion programs must account for the impact of both the promotion and the advertising when studying sales figures. Therefore, although sales are one indicator of effectiveness, they may be influenced by any number of intervening factors.

Advertisements that contain phone numbers, e-mail or Internet addresses, or response cards can be evaluated by measuring the number of people who respond. Internet responses are measured using "cookies," which make it possible for a firm to obtain considerable information about the person or business using a Web site. Many times, the person or business responding to a message is also willing to provide a great deal of personal information, voluntarily.

A second form of behavioral response is a test market. Test markets are used when a company examines the effects of a marketing effort on a small scale before launching a national or international advertising campaign. The primary advantage of using a test market is that an organization can examine several elements of an advertising program. If the test market is successful, then it is likely that the national or global campaign will also be effective. It is also an excellent method of testing a campaign in a new country before launching it full scale. Another advantage of a test market is that it resembles an actual situation more than any of the other tests. The key is to make sure that the site selected for the test market strongly resembles the target population. For example, if a product is targeted toward senior citizens, then it is important to conduct the study in an area that has a high concentration of senior citizens.

A test market can be as short as a few days or as long as two to three years. The longer the test market program runs, the more accurate will be the results. A test that is too short yields less reliable results. If the test market runs too long, the national market situation may change and the test market may no longer be a representative sample. The greatest problem with long test markets is that the competition is able to study what is going on, giving them time to react to the proposed advertising or marketing campaign.

Scanner data make it possible for results from test market campaigns to be quickly available. The figures can be studied to determine if test market results are acceptable. A firm can also design several versions of an advertising campaign in different test markets. Through scanner data, the firm can compare the sales from each test market to determine which version is the best. For example, in one test market, the firm may present an advertising campaign only. In a second test market, the firm may add coupons to the advertising program. In test market three, a premium and advertising can be used. Examining the results from each market helps the marketing team understand which type of campaign is most effective. (*See* EVALUATION CRITERIA FOR ADVERTISEMENTS *for additional information.*)

BENEFIT SEGMENTATION

A traditional marketing and advertising technique is to identify consumer groups with distinctive characteristics, and then to tailor marketing efforts to those groups. Benefit segmentation focuses on the advantages or benefits consumers receive from a product rather than the characteristics of the products themselves.

Benefit segmentation helps the advertising team understand what customers seek from a product. For example, benefit segmentation has been used in the fitness market. Regular exercisers belong in one of three benefit segments. The first group, called "winners," does whatever it takes to stay physically fit. This segment tends to be younger, upwardly mobile, and career oriented. The second group, "dieters," exercises to maintain weight control and physical appearance. This group tends to be females over the age of thirty-five. They are primarily interested in reliable wellness programs offered by hospitals and weight control nutritionists. The third group, "self-improvers," exercise to feel better and to control medical costs.[4] A fitness center can design a marketing program based on the profiles of the reasons why individuals exercise. In many cases, benefit segmentation is tied to other segmentation strategies, such as demographics or income levels.

BETTER BUSINESS BUREAU

The Better Business Bureau (BBB) system in the United States consists of a group of state offices. Each seeks to help nearly 24 million consumers and businesses each year with ethical and legal issues. The role of the BBB is to resolve disputes fairly through self-regulation and consumer education and to strengthen the bond of trust between businesses and consumers.

The BBB is a resource available to both consumers and businesses concerning unfair and deceptive advertising. The BBB compiles a summary of all charges leveled against individual firms. Customers can use this information to make judgments about the legitimacy of a company and its operations. The information is provided in carefully worded reports that raise cautionary flags when a firm has received a great number of complaints, and the general nature of customer concerns is revealed. The bureau helps individuals and business make sure they are dealing with a firm that has a low record of problems.

For allegations concerning false, misleading, or deceptive advertising, the BBB has instituted the National Advertising Division (NAD). The role of the NAD is to investigate complaints and determine the validity of the charges filed. If a complaint cannot be resolved by the NAD, it is referred to the National Advertising Review Board (NARB). The NARB works similarly to the Federal Trade Commission (FTC), but does not have any legal or regulatory power. However, most disputes are resolved by the NARB and few are passed onto the FTC for resolution. (*See both* NAD *and* NARB *for more information.*)

The BBB has also established the Children's Advertising Review Unit (CARU). This unit reviews complaints about children's advertising and provides industry self-regulation guidelines. It operates under operating procedures similar to those of the NAD except that it deals with all issues regarding children's advertising.

BRAND

A brand is the name that identifies a company, its goods, and/or its services. The goal of branding is to set a product apart from its competitors. Strong brands provide customers with assurances of quality and reduction of search time in the purchasing process. Brands have personalities. They include strengths, weaknesses, and flaws. Many brands produce family trees.

Market researchers seek to identify the "one thing" that the brand can stand for, that consumers will recognize, and that is salient to consumers. When these tasks are successfully completed, more powerful brand recognition occurs. Two important processes help establish stronger brand prestige. First, the brand name must be prominently promoted. Repetition is essential to capture the individual's attention and so that the message will be stored in his or her knowledge structures. Second, the brand name must be associated with its most prominent characteristic.[5]

Strong brands are especially important in mature markets, because few tangible distinctions exist between competing products. Any product improvement is quickly copied. Thus, only minor differences exist and in many product categories, even minor variations are hard to find. When brand names and labels are removed, consumers often cannot distinguish between brands. In those circumstances, having customers who know a brand name and are loyal to that brand can be the difference between success and failure.

The secret to a long brand life is finding one unique selling point and sticking with it. Companies that attempt to change the concept associated with a brand often create confusion among consumers and, in the long run, hurt the overall corporate image.

BRAND EQUITY

Brand equity is the set of characteristics that make a brand unique in the marketplace. Brand equity allows the company to charge a higher price and retain a market share that is greater than would otherwise be expected for an undifferentiated product. A strong brand gives power to the company as it deals with retailers. This power, in turn, leads to an improved position in terms of items such as shelf space and displays. Brand equity also influences wholesalers, affecting what they stock and which brands they encourage their customers to purchase. Wholesalers may stock several brands, but normally place greater emphasis on selling high-equity brands.

In business-to-business markets, brand equity often means it is possible to charge a higher price. Products with strong brand equity are often selected over products with low brand equity or brands that firms know little about. The same is true in international markets. Brand equity opens doors of foreign firms, brokers, and retailers and provides privileges that are not available to products with low brand equity. True brand equity keeps consumers from looking for cheaper products or from accepting special deals or incentives to buy other brands.

The basis of brand equity is brand recognition. A consumer must remember the brand name before equity can be developed. After brand recognition has been accomplished, the advertiser must create messages that express the product's unique selling point and seek to establish strong, positive consumer feelings.

Brand equity also includes domination, which is a view strongly held by consumers that the brand is number one in its product category. Domination may take place in a geographic region, or it may be present in a smaller product category or market niche. Domination can be associated with any product benefit that is desired by consumers. In each case, the brand must be viewed as number one in some way by consumers. For instance, with toothpastes, the brand consumers believe is the number one cavity fighter holds brand equity. For automobiles, the number one car in terms of safety is a strong brand as a result. The most critical aspect of maintaining brand equity is to keep delivering on promises.

BRAND EXTENSION

The use of an established brand name on goods or services that are not related to the core brand is brand extension. To leverage the equity built in its brands, firms will often enter new markets using a brand extension strategy. For example, Nike extended its brand name, which is associated with athletic shoes, to a line of clothing. Black & Decker extended the company's brand name, which is devoted to power tools, to a line of small kitchen appliances.

BRAND IMAGE

Brand image is the overall global attitude, feelings, and views a consumer or a business holds regarding a particular brand. An image starts with the product's attributes and includes intangibles such as feelings toward the brand. From the viewpoint of the brand, a highly reputable image generates many benefits:

- Extension of positive consumer feelings to new products
- The ability to charge a higher price or fee
- Consumer loyalty leading to more frequent purchases
- Positive word-of-mouth endorsements

Holding a strong brand image allows the company to develop additional goods and services. Since consumers are already familiar with the brand name and image, the introduction of a new product becomes much easier, as long-term customers are willing to give something new a try. Customers will normally transfer their trust in and beliefs about the known brand to a new product. Also, companies with favorable brand images often charge more for products since most customers believe they "get what they pay for." This, in turn, leads to better markup margins and greater profits.

Furthermore, brands with well-developed images have more loyal customers. A higher level of customer loyalty results in patrons purchasing more products over time. This is, in part, because less substitution purchasing takes place (such as when other companies offer discounts, sales, and other enticements to switch brands).

Advertising is a critical component in the effort to build brand image. Successful brands have two characteristics, being (1) "top of mind" and (2) the consumer's "top choice." When consumers are asked to identify brands that quickly come to mind from a product category, the brands identified are top of mind. When consumers are asked to pick the best or top brands in a category, these are top-choice brands. When a brand is both top of mind and top choice, it is likely to be the market leader.

BRAND MESSAGE STRATEGY

A message strategy is the primary tactic used in the creation of an advertising message. Message strategies can be divided into four categories: cognitive, affective, conative, and brand. Brand message strategies are designed to build or enhance the brand or corporate name in some way. Brand strategies can be placed into four subcategories:

- Brand user strategies
- Brand image strategies
- Brand usage strategies
- Corporate approaches

Brand user strategies are oriented to a type of individual. This individual uses a particular brand. One example of a brand user strategy involves celebrity endorsements. The idea is that consumers who like the celebrity will transfer that liking to the brand itself. Thus, basketball fans that like LeBron James may purchase the Nike brand. Perfume users who like Elizabeth Taylor may buy the White Diamonds brand. The endorsers who use the product cause consumers to recall the brand's name and develop a preference for that brand.

A brand image strategy is part of creating a brand's personality. The focus is on the brand rather than the user. Celebrities are often not used in brand image ads, and many times the ad does not even feature a person. A spokesperson appearing in an advertisement will normally be a typical person. Also, verbal copy will be limited. Instead, the brand name appears in the advertisement along with an Internet address and possibly a toll-free number.

Brand usage messages stress the different uses for a particular brand. The classic example of this approach is the Arm & Hammer baking soda commercials suggesting new uses of the product. These uses included reducing odors in a refrigerator or freezer and using the product for dental hygiene. Later the company promoted the use of the product to freshen carpets and reduce odors in cat litter boxes. Then, building on the brand name, Arm & Hammer developed its own lines of toothpaste and deodorant.

Corporate approaches center on the corporate name and image rather than individual brands. The goal is to develop goodwill or enhance the corporate name. The Allstate "good hands" claim is an example of a corporate approach.

BRAND PARITY

Brand parity occurs when consumers or businesses perceive that most goods or services within a product category are essentially the same. Multiple brands are available in practically every marketplace. Consumers typically believe the various brands have identical benefits. When consumers believe this, the result is brand parity. Under conditions of brand parity, shoppers purchase from a group of accepted brands rather than one specific brand. Quality is often not a major concern because consumers believe that any differences are minor. The result is that criteria such as price, availability, or a specific promotional deal have the biggest effect on the purchasing decision. In general, brand loyalty (the opposite of brand parity) has experienced a steady decline because of the proliferation of product choices.

To cope with brand parity problems, marketers generate messages designed to suggest that clear differences do exist. The goal is to build some type of perceived brand superiority for the company and its goods or services. Consumers are led to believe that a given company's products are not the same as the competition's. This task is often delegated to advertising.

BRAND POSITIONING

Brand positioning is the process of creating a perceptual map in the consumer's mind of the position of a particular brand relative to its competition. From a brand or corporate perspective, positioning can occur in the following ways:

- Attributes
- Competitors
- Use or application
- Price/quality relationship
- Product user
- Product class
- Cultural symbols

It is important to be sure that the chosen positioning strategy is relevant to consumers and provides them with a benefit that will be considered useful in decision making. Such an attribute for a deodorant may be that it will not cause allergic reactions. Clear differences can be stated to position a good or service away from those of competitors. The product itself may create a position by being clearly superior or offering a unique benefit. Many times, price/quality relationships establish the position of a product or a company. When a brand or a product becomes a cultural symbol, such as the Golden Arches of McDonald's, it has a strong position.

Brand positioning is a critical part of image and brand name management. Consumers have an extensive set of purchasing options. They can seek out products with specific advantages or attributes. Effective positioning, by whatever tactic chosen, can increase sales and strengthen the long-term positions of both individual products and the total organization. *(See the individual methods of brand positioning for additional information.)*

BRAND SPIRALING

The practice of using traditional media to promote and attract consumers to an online Web site is brand spiraling. Brand spiraling includes using television, radio, newspapers, magazines, billboards, and even simple shopping bags to encourage consumers to visit the firm's Web site.

The most common method of promoting a Web site is displaying the Web address on all printed and promotional materials. A second approach is to place the Web address in trade and consumer publications. Currently, more than 70 percent of U.S. companies register key words with search engines, because business buyers are often looking for a specific product. The odds of making a sale increase substantially when a firm's Web site is listed after a key word is typed into the search engine.

Companies with strong off line brands benefit from "halo effects." This means a well-known brand entices more customers to try new goods and services that are offered by the company on the Internet. The same customers are also more willing to provide information that can be used for greater personalization of messages. This halo effect results from the credibility of the firm's brand being transferred to an individual's evaluation of the Web site. Even though Barnes & Noble and Toys "R" Us were late entrants into e-commerce, both companies built successful Internet businesses because of the strong brand names that transferred to their Web site programs.

BRAND-LOYAL CONSUMERS

A brand-loyal consumer is someone who purchases only one particular brand and does not substitute regardless of any deal offered. One goal of marketing and advertising is to instill brand loyalty in as many customers as possible. A variety of techniques are possible; including differentiating the product; tying use of the product to a strongly held emotion, such as support of a family or a nation through patriotic feelings; and offering the best price/quality relationship.

It is not common for a customer to be either completely brand loyal or completely prone to being influenced by promotions. Purchase behaviors are best represented by a continuum anchored with promotion proneness at one end and brand loyalty at the other. People tend toward one approach but sometimes use the other approach. The tendency toward being brand loyal or promotion prone may depend on the product being purchased. The purchase of gasoline may be extremely promotion prone, whereas a car buyer may be quite brand loyal. Snack food purchases may be easily influenced by promotions. High-quality restaurants may have strongly brand-loyal clients.

BUSINESS BUYING CENTER

A business buying center is the group of individuals within a company that makes business purchase decisions. The buying center consists of five subsets of individuals playing various roles in the process. These roles can be performed by multiple individuals or, in the case of small firms, an individual may assume more than one role. The five roles involved in the buying center are

1. users,
2. buyers,
3. influencers,
4. deciders, and
5. gatekeepers.

Users are individuals within the buying center who use the product being considered. Buyers are the individuals who are given the official responsibility for making the purchase and negotiating the final terms of the deal. Influencers are individuals who influence the decision but are not direct users of the product. Deciders are the individuals who make the final decision about the product or the firm being chosen as the vendor. Gatekeepers are individuals who control the flow of information to members of the buying center. *(For more information about these roles, see each individual buying role.)*

BUSINESS-TO-BUSINESS BUYING PROCESS

In new-task purchasing situations, members of the buying center in a company go through seven steps in the business-to-business buying decision process:

1. Identification of a need
2. Establishment of specifications
3. Identification of alternatives
4. Identification of vendors

5. Evaluation of vendors
6. Selection of vendors
7. Negotiation of purchase terms

In new buy situations, all seven steps are completed. In modified re-buy or straight rebuy situations, one or more of the steps are eliminated. (*See* MODIFIED REBUY; NEW-TASK PURCHASE; *and* STRAIGHT REBUY *for additional information.*)

BUSINESS-TO-BUSINESS SEGMENTATION

Business-to-business (b-to-b) segmentation involves differentiating potential customers based on a market characteristic. The goal is to identify a homogenous group that will respond in like manner to an advertising message. The most common approaches to b-to-b segmentation include the following:

- NAICS/SIC code
- Size of business
- Geographic location
- Product usage

The North American Industry Classification System (NAICS) or Standard Industry Classification (SIC) codes aggregate firms by industry. This allows a business to target specific industries that purchase a type of products. As an example, ambulatory health care services are classified using the 623 code number. Any company offering products in that area can quickly develop a list of potential customers.

A second method of b-to-b segmentation is by the size of the business. Although some firms may target only large firms, others may cater to small or midsize firms. For example, an advertising agency may have the ability to serve small or midsize firms but not have the staff or resources to handle an international firm.

Geographic location is another method of segmentation. It is attractive to retail companies operating stores in specific locations, such as individual cities. It may also be applied to regions. Firms selling computer component parts could limit marketing programs to firms in the Silicon Valley in California.

Product usage can also be a method of segmentation. Aluminum is a common metal used in many industries. A firm that manufactures aluminum, however, may focus on specific industries such as companies that manufacture aluminum cans or the construction industry, which uses aluminum for buildings. By focusing on a specific usage of the product, the marketing department is better able to develop a strong brand name in selected market segments.

BUYER

The buyer is a member of the business buying center. A buyer has the formal responsibility of making the actual purchase. In larger organizations, there may be several buyers. These buyers are either purchasing agents or members of the purchasing department. In smaller organizations the buyer may be the owner or president of the company, a manager, or even a secretary. In addition to making the purchase, the buyer is usually responsible for working out all final details. The buyer will follow up to make sure delivery and purchase specifications have been met. (*See* BUSINESS BUYING CENTER *for additional information.*)

BUYING COMMUNITY

The buying community is an interlocking network of individual business owners and managers, trade organizations, social organizations, and small and medium-sized businesses. They are a valuable resource tool for small business owners to obtain pertinent business information in order to make better quality purchase decisions.

The buying community links small and medium-sized businesses and provides expert, reliable sources to them. This means a small business owner will be able to go outside of his or her business and obtain information to make informed purchasing decisions. In these situations, the influencers of the decisions are other business owners. The buying community is normally utilized for new task and modified rebuy purchase decisions. It is not useful in straight rebuy situations.

Smaller and medium-sized firms make purchases differently than larger organizations. The primary differences are in the areas of identifying, evaluating, and selecting vendors. Decision makers in smaller organizations tend to have less expertise and experience than those in larger firms. Also, members of small to medium-sized companies must play more of the buying center roles. This increases the risks associated with making purchasing decisions. Unfortunately, one bad decision can easily create a major financial crisis for the small company. Small and medium-size firms do not have the financial security to weather a poor decision. The expertise and advice provided by a buying community helps members of smaller firms avoid bad decisions.

CAMPAIGN DURATION

A principle of effective advertising is to identify the appropriate length for an advertising campaign. Using the same advertisement over a longer period of time helps embed the message in long-term memory. At the same time, an ad campaign that runs too long causes viewers to become bored, lose interest, and finally to ignore the ad. The goal is to make the campaign long enough to embed messages in viewers' long-term memories, but short enough that they do not become bored.

Reach and frequency are additional factors that affect the duration of a campaign. Reach is the number of people who see an advertisement. Frequency is the number of times the same person encounters the ad. Higher frequency usually leads to a shorter duration. Low reach may be associated with a longer duration. A typical advertising campaign lasts one to two months to optimize reach and frequency. (*See* FREQUENCY *and* REACH *for additional information.*)

CARRYOVER EFFECTS

When an advertised brand has generated an impact on consumers that is strong enough that the brand is remembered when the time comes to make a purchase, carryover effects are present. Durable goods such as refrigerators and televisions are purchased only when the need arises. The time between purchases is often years. Therefore, consumer decisions to buy such products will occur at any time. Advertisers of these types of products advertise continually in order to make sure consumers will either see ads just when they are in the market for the product or remember the company and the product due to the presence of carryover effects.

Decay effects occur when advertising is stopped. That is, fewer people will remember an advertisement as time passes after the ad stops running. To create carryover effects, advertising must be used on a regular basis. Sporadically advertising a product will usually not result in sufficient carryover effects to impact sales. (*See* DECAY EFFECTS; SALES-RESPONSE FUNCTION CURVE; *and* THRESHOLD EFFECT *for additional information.*)

CAUSE-RELATED MARKETING

Cause-related marketing is tying a marketing program to some type of charity work or program. This type of corporate or company altruism is based on the belief that consumers will purchase from companies who are willing to help a good cause. Surveys indicate that a significant number of consumers say they are willing to switch brands or retailers to firms that are associated with good causes. Other surveys suggest that consumers place high levels of trust in nonprofit organizations and prefer products marketed in association with nonprofit causes.

As a result, American businesses spend more than $600 million each year to buy the rights to use a nonprofit's name or logo in company advertising and marketing programs. Many consumers believe that brands associated with a nonprofit organization are superior to brands that are not tied to special causes.

In choosing a cause, a company's marketing team should focus on issues that relate to a specific business. Supporting such efforts is received more positively by consumers. When the company supports an unrelated cause, consumers may feel the business is simply trying to benefit from the nonprofit's reputation. This may lead some consumers to stop buying the company's products. Consumers are becoming skeptical about the motives behind the increased emphasis being given to various charities. Although most people understand that a business must benefit from the relationship, they still tend to hold negative views when they believe that the business is exploiting a relationship with a nonprofit.

CEASE AND DESIST ORDER

A cease and desist order is issued by the Federal Trade Commission (FTC) when it concludes that a company has produced an advertisement or marketing communication piece that is misleading, deceptive, or unfair. When an FTC judge concludes that a violation of the law has occurred, a cease and desist order is prepared. The order requires the company to immediately stop the disputed practice and refrain from similar practices in the future. If the company's management group is not satisfied with the ruling by the administrative law judge, the case can be appealed to the full FTC commission. The full commission holds hearings similar to those presented before administrative law judges. Rulings are made after hearing evidence and testimony. Companies not satisfied with the ruling of the full FTC commission can appeal the case to the U.S. Court of Appeals. The highest level of appeal is the U.S. Supreme Court. The danger for companies that appeal cases to the Court of Appeals is that consumer redress can be sought at that point. In other words, companies found guilty of violating laws can be ordered to pay civil penalties.

CHILDREN'S ADVERTISING

Advertising to children is a controversial area of marketing. By the time a child turns three years old, it is likely the child will be able to recognize McDonald's Golden Arches. Children may also have learned brand names such as Pepsi, Pizza Hut, and Toys "R" Us. Critics of advertising to children contend that by the time a child reaches middle school, many teens are strongly brand conscious. Teens believe they can only wear certain brands of clothing if they want to be accepted by peers.

Several advocacy groups oppose the current freedom companies have to advertise to children, especially preschool children. The most extreme position is that ads directed at children should be banished completely. This argument is based on the view that children do not have the mental ability to correctly interpret advertisements. Thus, marketers are able to take advantage of a child's inability to weigh evidence and make an informed decision. Other groups do not favor eliminating advertising to children but do support limits and regulations.

The other extreme position is that the First Amendment protects advertising. Any type of regulation would therefore be an infringement of a constitutional right to free speech. In the future, Congress may seek to resolve this issue through additional legislation, especially as Internet advertising proliferates.

It is the role of the Federal Communications Commission (FCC) to monitor advertising directed to children. Under current law, television stations are limited to 12 minutes of children's advertising per hour during the weekdays and 10.5 minutes per hour on weekends. The content of children's ads is regulated by the Federal Trade Commission.

The Better Business Bureau established the Children's Advertising Review Unit (CARU) to deal with issues pertaining to children's advertising. The CARU's role is to provide industry regulation of children's advertising and to ensure that companies have established guidelines to follow. Although the CARU has no regulatory or legal power, it has been a strong voice within the advertising industry in promoting children's concerns.

CLUTTER

Clutter exists when consumers are exposed to hundreds of marketing messages per day. The result is that most ads are mentally tuned out. Some examples of clutter include

- a series of six to ten advertisements within each cluster of television ads,
- eight to ten minutes of advertising per thirty-minute television show,
- more than 50 percent of the pages of a magazine containing advertisements, and
- multiple billboards that seldom change content.

The challenge for advertisers is to find a way to break through the clutter and get noticed. Advertising and marketing communications programs are designed to attract attention to overcome clutter and then to making compelling appeals that lead to purchases.

CO-BRANDING

When two brands are woven together to prepare a single product offering, it is a co-branding effort. Examples include Subway sandwich shops within convenience stores, Little Caesars in K-Mart outlets, and McDonald's units in Wal-Mart stores. Co-branding can take three forms: ingredient branding, cooperative branding, and complementary branding.

Ingredient branding means that one brand is placed within another. Intel processors placed inside of Dell, IBM, and Compaq computers are perhaps the most famous form of ingredient branding. Cooperative branding is the joint venture of two brands, such as Subway located in 7-Eleven convenience stores. Complementary branding is the marketing of two brands together, with each maintaining its own identity. For example, an advertisement promoting both the Gateway Arch and St. Louis Cardinals baseball team is a complementary approach, since both can be visited in the same nearby location. Busch Gardens is often promoted in conjunction with other attractions in Florida. A classic complementary branding approach is Seagram's 7 and 7UP, attached by the phrase "7 and 7."

COCOONING

One response to busy and hectic consumer lifestyles is cocooning. The stress of long working hours accompanied by long commuting times has led many individuals to retreat and cocoon in their homes. Cocooning is making the home environment as soothing as possible. Evidence of cocooning includes

- major expenditures on elaborate homes;
- extensive and expensive sound systems;
- satellite systems with big-screen televisions;
- swimming pools, saunas, and hot tubs;

- gourmet kitchens with large dining rooms;
- decks and porches; and
- moving to the country or to a gated theme community.

Many advertisements now emphasize cocooning aspects of goods and services, especially because of the terrorist attacks of September 11, 2001. Internet ads will sometimes focus on the utility of shopping at home during the Christmas season by offering the consumer a method to avoid the hustle and bustle of the holidays.

COGNITIVE (COMPONENT OF ATTITUDE)

Attitude is a mental position related to a topic, person, event, object, company, or product that influences the person's feelings, perceptions, learning processes, and subsequent behaviors and consists of three components: affective, cognitive, and conative.

The cognitive component is the person's mental images, understanding, and interpretations of the person, object, issue, or product. In developing an attitude toward a product or brand, the most common sequence of events that takes place is:

cognitive > affective > conative

In other words, a person first develops an understanding of or knowledge about a product. This may result from exposure to the product or to information from other sources, such as advertising, the Internet, or a referral from a friend. Eventually, these thoughts become either positive or negative. Positive or negative evaluations are made regarding companies, brands, goods, and services.

In terms of advertising, the goal is to provide consumers with knowledge about the product (cognitive). Once this achieved, the objective is to move the consumer to develop feelings and emotional ties with the product (the affective) that result in the actual purchase (the conative).

COGNITIVE DISSONANCE

Consumers often experience doubt after making a purchase. This is known as postpurchase cognitive dissonance. It can result from situations in which there is a high degree of involvement, a socially visible purchasing experience, or if the good or service is expensive. Cognitive dissonance is most likely to appear when the consumer spends a greater amount of time searching for information and evaluating the different alternatives. Extra investments of time, money, or ego make it natural for a consumer to question a decision after it has been made.

Consumers will pay attention to advertisements and other marketing materials after a purchase to reduce the tension or sense of disharmony associated with cognitive dissonance. Marketing communications, along with other endorsements and reassurances (including those made by the sales agent), can help the individual believe a good decision was made.

In making postpurchase evaluations, consumers often compare the brand they selected with the brands they did not. If they have just made a tough decision, and two or three other brands could have been purchased, dissonance may arise. Also, the consumer may see advertisements by the competitor and none by the firm selling the chosen brand. If so, this too will increase the level of dissonance.

The marketing team can reduce cognitive dissonance through postpurchase assurance. Follow-up remarks suggesting the consumer made a wise choice, exposures to additional advertisements, and quality servicing can all help to alleviate cognitive dissonance. For some major purchases, such as automobiles or houses, the selling agent may actually call or visit the customer to provide additional postpurchase assurance.

COGNITIVE MAPPING

Cognitive mapping is the manner in which consumers store information in the brain and relate that information to previous experiences and other memories. Knowing how people store, retrieve, and evaluate information is a useful tool for creatives developing advertising messages.

Cognitive maps are simulations of the knowledge structures embedded in an individual's brain. These structures contain a person's assumptions, beliefs, interpretations of facts, feelings, and attitudes. Individuals utilize knowledge structures to help them interpret new information and to determine appropriate responses to fresh information or a novel situation. Each piece of information is connected by linkages to other nodes of information, forming a complex mental structure. These structures allow a person to function and relate new information to current information. Cognitive maps usually consist of multiple layers and levels of information.

From an advertising perspective, it is easier to strengthen cognitive linkages that already exist. Adding new linkages or modifying linkages is much more difficult. For example, if a consumer believes a certain brand of toothpaste is good at whitening teeth, it is easier to strengthen that linkage than to create a new linkage that the toothpaste is good for whitening or to change a current belief if the consumer does not believe the toothpaste is good for whitening.

To achieve the best results, creatives design ads that reach the linkages consumers have already made between a product and other key ideas. Common linkages exist between products and ideas such as convenience, quality, value, cost, fun, sexy, dangerous, practical, exotic, and many others. Carefully planned advertising campaigns seek out linkages that entice the consumer to buy a given product and to believe in (or be loyal to) that product in the future.

COGNITIVE MESSAGE STRATEGY

A message strategy is the primary tactic used in the creation of an advertising message. Message strategies can be divided into four categories: cognitive, affective, conative, and brand. In the development of an advertisement, a cognitive message strategy utilizes rational arguments or information. The advertisement's key message is focused on the product's attributes or the benefits customers will obtain from using the product. For example, life insurance may be described as caring, thoughtful, or being loving toward one's family. An appliance may be shown as durable, convenient, or handy to use. Services such as online airline or hotel reservations are often portrayed as being the frugal way to travel. Cognitive message strategies should make these benefits clear to potential customers. There are five major forms of cognitive strategies:

1. Generic
2. Preemptive
3. Unique selling proposition
4. Hyperbole
5. Comparative

A generic message strategy is a direct promotion of a product's attributes or benefits without any claim of superiority. A preemptive message strategy is a claim of superiority on a specific product attribute or benefit. A unique selling proposition is an explicit, testable claim of uniqueness or superiority that can be supported or substantiated by independent tests. A hyperbole message strategy is an untestable claim of superiority about a specific product attribute or benefit. A comparative message strategy will directly or indirectly compare a product to one or more of its competitors. *(See each type of cognitive message strategy for additional information.)*

COMMUNICATION

Communication is the creation, transmission, reception, and processing of information. When a person, group, or organization transmits an idea or message, the receiver (another person or group) must be able to effectively process that information. Communication occurs when the message that was sent reaches its destination in a form that is understood by the intended audience.

COMMUNICATION MARKET ANALYSIS

One important step in an advertising and communications program is to assess the organization's strengths and weaknesses in the area of marketing communication and combine that information with an analysis of opportunities and threats, which are present in the firm's external environment. The communication market analysis process is designed to help the marketing team make this assessment. It is similar to a managerial approach called SWOT analysis (strengths, weaknesses, opportunities, threats). A communication market analysis typically has five components:

1. Competitive analysis
2. Opportunity analysis
3. Target market analysis
4. Analysis of customers
5. Positioning analysis

A competitive analysis should identify the firm's major competitors. Opportunities are revealed in situations in which the firm can focus advertising and promotional efforts on company strengths and opportunities in the marketplace. A target market analysis identifies key target markets by using segmentation or some other approach. An analysis of customers reveals how well the firm's previous marketing communications efforts have been received by the public as well as by other businesses and potential customers. A positioning analysis explains how the firm and its products are perceived relative to the competition. The goal of a communications analysis is to help the account executive, creative, and others focus on key markets and customers. The program should help each member of the advertising team understand how the firm is currently competing in the marketplace. Then the team is better able to establish and pursue specific advertising objectives.

In addition, for the purposes of advertising, two important items should be defined as part of the communication market analysis:

1. The media usage habits of the target market
2. The media utilized by the competition

Knowing media usage habits is vital because various market segments have differences in when and how they view various media. For example, older blacks watch television programs in patterns that are quite different from older whites. Males watch more sports programs than females, and so forth.

Media usage habits are also important in assessing business-to-business markets. It is important to determine the trade journals or business publications the various members of the buying center would most likely read. Engineers, who tend to be influencers, will have different media viewing habits than vice presidents, who may be deciders. Discovering which media will reach a target market (and which will not) is a key part of a communication market analysis.

Furthermore, the advertising team must understand how media are used by competitors. To be successful, it is important to respond to advertising claims made by competitors and to make certain messages are finding the right audience. Competitor ads may point out a new venue for reaching the targeted audience.

COMPARATIVE MESSAGE STRATEGY

A message strategy is the primary tactic used in the creation of an advertising message. Message strategies can be divided into four categories: cognitive, affective, conative, and brand. The cognitive message strategies, in turn, can be divided into five subcategories: generic, preemptive, unique selling proposition, hyperbole, and comparative.

An advertisement with a comparative message strategy means the advertiser is directly or indirectly comparing a good or service to the competition. The competitor may or may not be mentioned by name in the advertisement. An advertiser may infer the competitor through a subtle message or symbol, or present a "make-believe" competitor, giving it a name such as product X. This approach, however, is not as effective for comparative advertising as stating the actual competitor's name. At the same time, advertising agencies must be sure to substantiate any claims made concerning the competition.

Comparative ads often capture the attention of consumers. This can enhance both brand and message awareness. Furthermore, consumers tend to remember more of what the ad said about a brand than if the same information was given in a noncomparative ad format. At the same time, comparative ads may negatively affect consumer attitudes. Many consumers think comparative ads are less believable. They view the information about the sponsor brand as being exaggerated and conclude that the information about the comparison brand is probably being misstated or misrepresents the competitor.

Viewers can acquire negative attitudes toward the advertisement, which are, in turn, transferred to the sponsor's product. This is especially true when the sponsor runs a negative comparative ad. The form of advertisement portrays the competition's product in a negative light. The concept of "spontaneous trait transference" suggests that if someone suggests another person has a negative trait, other people will tend to remember the speaker as having that trait. In a comparative ad, when the comparison brand is criticized based upon some particular attribute, viewers of the ad may attribute that deficiency to the sponsor brand as well.[6] This is most likely to occur when the comparative brand and not the sponsored brand is being used by the consumer.

Comparative message strategies should be used with caution. The comparison brand must be picked carefully to ensure that consumers see it is a viable comparable brand. Actual product attributes and customer benefits must be used, without stretching the information or providing misleading information. The differences must be real and important. When comparisons are misleading, the FTC may step in to investigate. The largest category of complaints dealt with by the FTC is in the area of comparative advertising. In general, comparing a less well-known brand to the market leader seems to work the best.

COMPETITIVE ANALYSIS

The goal of conducting a competitive analysis is to identify a firm or brand's major competitors. This includes who the competition is and what they are doing in the areas of advertising and communication. To assess the competition, advertisers need to study the advertising tactics used by the competition to gain a better understanding of how the competition attacks the marketplace. It is important to identify what potential customers are seeing, hearing, and reading about the competition.

After reviewing the advertising approach used by competing firms, a competitive analysis continues with the collection of secondary data. The first items to look for are statements the competition makes about themselves. Sources of secondary data about competitors can be found in

- advertisements,
- promotional materials,
- annual reports,
- a prospectus for a publicly held corporation, and
- Web sites.

Final assessment continues with studying what other people are saying about the competition. Trade journals, visits with vendors and suppliers who have dealt with the competition or who have read the competition's literature, and a review of news articles and press releases regarding competitor activities provide additional insights. The importance of the final step is to discover how companies close to the competition view them. This gives the advertising team a sense of how the brand or product is being compared with the competition.

COMPETITOR POSITIONING STRATEGY

Positioning is the process of creating a perception in the mind of consumers concerning the nature of a brand relative to the competition. Possible positioning approaches include attributes, competitors, use or application, price-quality, product user, product class, and cultural symbol. Using competitors to garner a position in the consumer's mind is a common positioning tactic. The competition may already be present in the cognitive maps of many consumers. Creating an additional link to a company or brand along with a favorable comparison point should help the consumer recall the new brand and think positively about it. This strategy is successful when an advertiser is trying to be considered with a competitor within a consumer's cognitive map. Comparing new or relatively unknown brands to market leaders is an excellent positioning strategy because the goal is to provide an alternative choice and also for the consumer to think of the new or unknown brand within the same context as the market leader. (*See* COGNITIVE MAPPING *for additional information.*)

COMPLEMENTARY BRANDING

Complementary branding is a form of co-branding. It is the marketing of two brands together to encourage coconsumption or copurchases such as Oreo milkshakes being sold in Dairy Queen stores. For example, a tie-in between a snack food and a soft drink would be complementary branding.

COMPREHENSION TEST

Comprehension tests are used to evaluate the effectiveness of completed advertisements or even advertisements that are still in the production stage. During the concept testing phase as well as after an ad has appeared, a comprehension test would involve asking participants the meaning of an advertisement. The goal is to make sure that participants correctly understand or interpret the message that creatives want to convey. In a comprehension test the moderator can explore reasons why an intended message is comprehended correctly or why it is not.

CONATIVE (COMPONENT OF ATTITUDE)

An attitude is a mental position taken toward a topic, person, event, object, company, or product that influences the person's feelings, perceptions, learning processes, and subsequent behaviors and consists of three components: affective, cognitive, and conative. Decision and action tendencies are the conative parts of attitude. In most cases, actions follow the cognitive and affective components of attitude. Thus, before a consumer purchases a product, the individual must have knowledge that the product exists and develop a positive attitude toward the product and brand. Then the consumer takes action and buys the item.

Some purchases require little thought, have a low price, or do not require a great deal of emotional involvement. In those circumstances the consumer may go ahead and purchase the product without any other thought process. Then, as a result of the consumption experience, cognitive and affective evaluations of the brand are formed after the action (buying the product) has already taken place.

For instance, while shopping for groceries, a consumer sees a new brand of snack crackers on sale. The person may have never even seen the brand or product type before. However, the item is on sale, so the customer decides to give it a try. As the consumer eats the crackers, an understanding of the taste, texture, and other qualities of the product emerges. The consumer reads the package to learn more about contents, including how many calories are in each serving. Eventually the buyer develops feeling toward the crackers that affect future purchases of the brand.

CONATIVE MESSAGE STRATEGY

A message strategy is the primary tactic used in the creation of an advertising message. Message strategies can be divided into four categories: cognitive, affective, conative, and brand. Conative message strategies are designed to lead consumers to some type of consumer behavior. The behavior may be to redeem a coupon, access an Internet site, place an order, or inquire about a particular product. Advertisements can be designed to elicit such behavior. Thus, conative strategies are present in television advertisements promoting music CDs or cassettes when the ad seeks to persuade viewers to call a toll-free number to purchase the item. The advertisement may also encourage the action by mentioning that the CD cannot be purchased at stores and is available for only a limited time. Conative message strategies consist of two types:

1. Action-inducing message strategies
2. Promotional message strategies

In action-inducing advertisements the goal of the ad is to induce or encourage consumers to perform some type of action, such as calling a toll-free number, accessing a Web site, or making a trial purchase. In promotional message advertisements the message or copy supports some type of trade or consumer promotion. For instance, the ad may promote a sweepstakes offer and the prizes that can be won or a coupon for 50 cents off the purchase price.

CONCEPT TESTING

Part of testing an advertisement is devoted to making sure the message is correctly sent and interpreted. Concept testing is a message evaluation technique aimed at the actual content of the ad and is designed to discover the impact of the content on potential customers. Concept tests can be used for advertisements as well as other promotional pieces.

Concept tests are used to test ideas (or concepts) in the early stages of an advertisement's development rather than after an actual commercial has been taped. Changes can then be made when it is less costly to do so. After the advertisement has already been created, it is much more expensive to make changes. Also, once an ad is finished, creatives and others who worked on it feel a sense of ownership and are more resistant to making changes.

Focus groups are often used in concept tests. Advertisers normally use independent marketing research firms to conduct focus groups rather than performing them internally. This helps prevent biased results. An independent company is more likely to report that a certain advertising approach did not work than someone who developed the approach and has a vested interest in it. Several components of an advertisement can be evaluated with concept tests:

- The copy or verbal component of an advertisement
- The message and its meaning
- The translation of copy in an international advertisement
- The effectiveness of peripheral cues, such as product placement in the ad and props used
- The value associated with an offer or prize in a contest

Two common testing instruments used in concept tests are called comprehension and reaction tests. Comprehension tests assess the meaning of an advertisement. The idea is to make sure viewers correctly comprehend the message. When the message is misinterpreted, it is possible to discover the reasons why the intended message was not comprehended correctly by the individual or the group. Reaction tests measure overall feelings about an advertisement, most notably whether the response is negative or positive. When consumers or participants in a focus group react negatively to an ad or particular copy in an ad, changes can be made before the ad is developed. It is possible for an advertisement to be correctly comprehended but elicit negative emotions. Exploring any negative feelings provides creatives with inputs to modify the ad.

CONJUNCTIVE HEURISTICS

Conjunctive heuristics is a purchasing decision model that establishes a minimum or threshold rating that brands must meet in order to be considered. For example, in the purchase of an automobile, a consumer may decide the vehicle has to be rated for at least twenty five miles per gallon in terms of fuel consumption. Any vehicle that does not meet this minimum threshold is eliminated from consideration. For a business buyer looking for a shipping company, a minimum threshold may be that the shipping company must offer both rail and truck shipping capabilities. Only firms that offer both will be considered.

CONSENT ORDER

The Federal Trade Commission (FTC) is responsible for investigating complaints concerning false and misleading advertising. At the initial stages, the investigation is kept confidential to protect the FTC and the company being investigated. If the FTC concludes the law has been violated, a consent order is issued. In signing the consent order, the company agrees to stop the disputed practice without any admission of guilt. In most of the investigations by the FTC in which false and misleading advertising is found, companies agree to the consent order and the matter ends. If the company does not agree to the consent order or continues the false or misleading practice, the FTC issues an administrative complaint, which means that the case will be heard by an administrative law judge.

CONSTRAINT

The last component of a creative brief is an outline of advertising constraints. These constraints come from any legal or mandatory restrictions placed on messages. Constraints include legal protection of trademarks, logos, and copy restrictions. Other constraints may be associated with warranties and the disclaimers that accompany warranties. For example, a tire warranty will normally specify "under normal driving conditions" as part of the guarantee of the product.

Another form of constraint is anything that is legally imposed. The Surgeon General's warnings on alcohol and cigarettes are examples of constraints. Nutritional claims and lists of ingredients are also constraints in some circumstances, especially in the packaging of foods. (*See* CREATIVE BRIEF *for additional information.*)

CONSUMER DECISION-MAKING PROCESS

The consumer decision-making process involves five steps:

1. Problem recognition
2. Information search
3. Evaluation of alternatives
4. The purchase decision
5. Postpurchase evaluation

Problem recognition occurs when a consumer's desired state is different than his or her actual state. In other words, the consumer recognizes a need or a want. For example, a person who has not eaten will recognize a need to either purchase some food or prepare a meal. This need can be triggered by actual hunger pains or through seeing an advertisement on television or on a billboard.

Once a need or want has been recognized, the consumer is ready to search for information. The first stage is to conduct an internal search for information that is already stored in the brain. Often the problem can be solved with internal information. If this is not sufficient or if the consumer desires additional information, then an external search is conducted. The extent of the external search depends on factors such as the person's level of involvement with the purchase decision, his or her past experience, and level of shopping enthusiasm.

The third step in the purchase process is the evaluation of alternatives that are generated from the information search. The common methods of evaluating alternatives are the evoked set method, the multiattribute model, and affect referral. In the evoked set method, the consumer chooses alternatives that are part of his or her evoked, or acceptable, set of alternatives. With the multiattribute approach, a consumer evaluates alternatives on a number of attributes and chooses the brand that has the highest overall score. With affect referral, the consumer chooses the brand he or she likes the best.

From the evaluation of alternatives, the purchase decision is made. In most cases the consumer selects the alternative that is evaluated as best or highest. On some occasions, however, the purchase decision differs from the evaluation of alternatives. For example, a consumer may have decided on a certain brand of scanner or computer, but when he or she arrives at the store a special promotion on a different brand or a conversation with the sales rep may change the person's mind. As a result, a different brand is purchased.

The last step is the postpurchase evaluation. For expensive purchases or highly visible products, a consumer is likely to spend some time evaluating whether or not a good decision was made. For low-involvement products, such as a pair of socks or food items such as sugar, little time is spent on postpurchase evaluation. If the product performed adequately, the information is stored in the person's memory for future internal searches when the need once again arises.

CONSUMER PROMOTION

Consumer promotions are the incentives aimed at a firm's customers. They are also called sales promotions. The target customers are end users of the good or service or other businesses that consume the good or service. Consumer promotions are directed toward individuals or firms that will be using the product, and the product is not resold to another business, which means they are used in consumer markets and business-to-business markets. The most common consumer promotions are

- coupons,
- premiums,
- contests and sweepstakes,
- refunds and rebates,
- sampling,
- bonus packs, and
- price-offs.

CONTESTS AND SWEEPSTAKES

Contests and sweepstakes are a type of consumer sales promotion. There are differences between contests and sweepstakes that are primarily legal distinctions. In a contest, participants are required to perform some type of activity. The winner is selected based on who performs best or provides the most correct answers. Often, contests require a participant to make a purchase to enter. In some states, however, it is illegal to require consumers to make purchases in order to enter contests. Both state and national laws apply to contests.

In a sweepstakes, no purchase is required to enter. Consumers may enter as many times as they wish. It is legal to restrict customers to one entry per visit to the store or some other location. In a sweepstakes, the chances of winning are based on a probability factor. The probability of winning must be clearly stated on all point-of-purchase displays and advertising materials. In a sweepstakes, the probability of winning each prize must be published in advance. This means the firm must know how many winning tickets, as compared to total tickets, have been prepared.

Contests and sweepstakes are used in both consumer and business markets. They are designed to create repeat business and bring additional traffic to a location. They also can heighten awareness of a product or a company.

CONTINUITY

Three types of exposure patterns are used in advertising: continuous, pulsating, and discontinuous. In a continuous exposure pattern or schedule, media buys are made in a steady stream over the life of the campaign. For instance, a continuous schedule means a company purchased ad space in specific magazines over a period of one to two years. At the same time, the company will rotate advertisements so that readers do not become bored with one particular ad. The goal of a continuous pattern of exposure is to create long-term familiarity with a brand, product, or company such that a buyer will recall the firm when it is time to make a purchase. Thus, an athletic shoe company may be likely to continuously buy advertising space in various runners' magazines as well as other magazines focusing on physical fitness to enhance the brand. Consumers purchase athletic shoes as they wear out, which is a random schedule based on how much usage the shoes receive. Thus, recall of the brand at the time of purchase is crucial.

COOPERATIVE ADVERTISING PROGRAM

Cooperative advertising is a component of trade promotions called vendor support programs, which are offers to support a retailer, wholesaler, or agent's programs. In a cooperative advertising program, one company agrees to reimburse another a certain percentage of advertising costs. For example, a manufacturer that creates a component for another product, such as a Pentium processor for a computer, may pay part of the computer company's advertising costs in order to promote the processor. Intel utilizes such a cooperative advertising program with many computer manufacturers.

To receive reimbursement, specific guidelines concerning the placement of the ad and its content must be followed. In almost all cases, no competing products can be advertised and the brand must be prominently displayed. There may be other restrictions on how the brand is advertised as well as specific photos or copy that must be used.

Each year, an estimated $25 billion in co-op money is offered by manufacturers to retailers, of which only about two-thirds is claimed.[7] Some of the more common reasons that advertising allocation dollars are not claimed include the following:

- Co-op claims are rejected by the manufacturer because of errors in filing.
- Purchase accruals are tracked inaccurately.
- Retailers are unaware of a co-op program.
- Restrictions placed by the manufacturer are not followed correctly.

Although errors do occur in the filing of claims, the more common reasons for not collecting are that purchase accrual records are not kept accurately and retailers are simply unaware that a cooperative program is in place.

COOPERATIVE BRANDING

Cooperative branding is a form of co-branding, in which there is a joint venture of two or more brands into a new good or service. For example, Citibank may offer a MasterCard that is tied in with American Airlines. The three companies form a joint venture to produce a special credit card. The intent of cooperative branding is to build on the strength of all of the brands involved.

COPYTESTING

Copytesting is a message evaluation methodology that is used when an advertisement is finished or in its final stages of development prior to production. The tests are designed to solicit responses to the main message of the ad as well as the format in which that message is being presented. For a television ad, a copytest could be conducted using a storyboard format or a version that is filmed by agency members rather than professional actors.

The two most common copytesting techniques are portfolio and theater tests. Both of these tests place the test advertisement with other advertisements, usually within a magazine or documentary film. A portfolio test is a display of a set of print ads, one of which is the ad being evaluated. A theater test is a display of a set of television ads, including the one being evaluated. The individuals who participate in these studies do not know which piece is under scrutiny. Portfolio and theater tests mimic reality in the sense that consumers are often exposed to multiple messages. Most television programs include commercial breaks in which a series of commercials is shown. The same is true for radio programming.

Copytests allow researchers to compare a target piece with other marketing messages. For these approaches to yield the optimal findings, it is essential that all of the advertisements shown are in the same stage of development (e.g., a set of storyboards or a series of nearly completed coupon offers).

The various forms of copytesting programs include focus groups as well as other measurement devices. An ad or coupon that is in the final stage of design can be tested using the mall intercept technique, in which researchers stop and question people who are shopping in a mall. The shoppers are asked to evaluate the advertising piece.

The mall intercept technique can include a portfolio approach as well. To do so, subjects are asked to examine an advertisement that is mixed in with others, normally six to ten ads, coupons, or other marketing communications pieces. Comprehension and reaction tests are then used.

CORPORATE ADVERTISING

When an advertisement emphasizes the name and image of a corporation rather than an individual brand, the approach is called corporate advertising. Corporate advertisements have many purposes. They may be used to build brand image or recognition, especially when the name of the corporation has changed following a merger or takeover.

Due to the increasing importance of creating and building a positive image, corporate advertising is becoming a more widespread advertising strategy. This is especially true because consumer trust has become a key issue. In the first few years of the new millennium, many noteworthy corporate failures took place in organizations such as Enron and Arthur Andersen. Consumer distrust of corporations began to rise. One key goal of corporate advertising is to build trust along with a positive image of the organization.

Social responsibility advertising is another example of corporate advertising. Thus, if a firm emphasizes how it helps students in a classroom learning program, the advertisement is utilizing a corporate approach. (*See* CORPORATE IMAGE *and* SOCIAL RESPONSIBILITY ADVERTISING *for additional information.*)

CORPORATE IMAGE

A corporate image is the sum of everything a corporation stands for or represents in the marketplace. Image includes all tangible as well as intangible facets of the corporation. From a customer's perspective, a corporate image consists of the overall, global feelings and attitude toward a company. Image is also important in business-to-business relationships. For example, a hotel with a positive image may experience substantial return visits by business travelers as well as consumers on vacation.

The goal of managing a corporate image is to create a stable, positive impression in the minds of clients and customers. Perceptions of a company's image may vary from person to person or business to business. The overall or most general image of a firm is determined by the conglomerate view of all publics. Customers are influenced by image both positively and negatively.

A corporate image contains many invisible and intangible elements. Tangible elements include company products and policies. Intangible elements are created by consumer or business perceptions. Negative events and resulting perceptions can stain or damage the firm's long-term, overall image.

From a consumer's perspective, a positive corporate image serves several useful functions:

- Assurance regarding purchase decisions of familiar products in unfamiliar settings
- Assurance concerning purchases in which there is little previous experience
- Reduction of search time in purchase decisions
- Psychological reinforcement and social acceptance

From the viewpoint of the firm, a positive, well-defined corporate image generates the following benefits:

- Extension of positive feelings by customers to new products
- The ability to charge a higher price or fee
- Consumer loyalty leading to more frequent purchases
- Positive word-of-mouth communications
- The ability to attract quality employees
- More favorable ratings by financial observers and analysts

CORPORATE LOGO

A corporate logo is used in conjunction with a corporate name. The goal in creating a corporate logo is to make sure it says or represents the correct image for the company. Corporate names and logos can aid in memory recall of specific brands and even specific advertisements. They aid consumers in retail stores by making shopping easier and faster. Pictures and images such as those found in logos are processed in the mind faster than words. Consequently, search time is reduced when consumers can look for products that are identified by distinctive logos.

Quality logos should meet four tests. First, they should be easily recognizable. Second, they should be familiar. Third, they should elicit a consensual meaning among those in the firm's target market, and, finally, they should evoke positive feelings.

To be advantageous to companies, logo recognition must occur at two levels. First, consumers must remember seeing the logo in the past. It must be stored in memory and, when it is seen at the store, the memory is jogged. Second, the logo must remind consumers of the brand or corporate name. This reminder should elicit positive feelings regarding either the brand name or corporate manufacturer.

CORRECTIVE ADVERTISING

In rare and severe cases involving deceptive, false, or misleading advertisements, the Federal Trade Commission (FTC) may order a firm to prepare and run a series of corrective advertisements. A corrective advertisement is designed to bring consumers back to the neutral point or position they held prior to viewing a false, misleading, or deceptive advertisement. Corrective ads are only required when the FTC concludes that consumers have been so misled that discontinuing the misleading ads is not sufficient to remedy the situation.

COST PER RATING POINT

The cost per rating point (CPRP) is a relative measure of the efficiency of media vehicle relative to a firm's target market. The formula for calculating cost per rating point is:

CPRP = cost of media buy ÷ vehicle's rating

The vehicle's rating is the percentage of a firm or brand's target market that is exposed to the media vehicle. To illustrate, assume the cost of a four-color advertisement in *People* magazine is $605,800 and that the total readership of *People* at the time the ad is placed is 21,824,000. Not all of the readers, however, fit into the target market. In this case, of the 21,824,000 readers, only 1,964,000 fit into the advertiser's target audience. This yields a rating of 9.0 (1,964,000 ÷ 21,824,000). Plugging the rating of 9.0 into the above formula yields a CPRP of $67,311:

$$\$605,800 \div 9.0 = \$67,311$$

COST PER THOUSAND

Cost per thousand (CPM) is the dollar cost of reaching 1,000 members of a media vehicle's audience. The formula to calculate the cost per thousand is:

$$CPM = (\text{cost of media buy} \div \text{total audience}) \times 1,000$$

To illustrate, suppose the cost of running a four-color advertisement in a magazine is $965,940. Furthermore, assume the readership of that magazine is 13,583,000 readers. Therefore, the CPM is $71.11. This value was calculated in the following manner.

$$(\$965,940 \div 13,583,000) \times 1,000 = \$71.11$$

COUPON

A coupon is one type of price reduction offer presented to consumers. Coupons may offer a percentage off the retail price such as 25 percent or 40 percent, or an absolute amount (50 cents or $1.00). In the United States, more than 300 billion coupons are distributed annually and 4.8 billion are redeemed each year. This 2 percent redemption rate represents approximately $3.6 billion in savings for consumers. The average value is 70.2 cents per coupon. Approximately

78 percent of all U.S. households use coupons and 64 percent are willing to switch brands with coupons.

Nearly 80 percent of all coupons are distributed by manufacturers. Some 88 percent of all coupons are sent out through print media, with 80 percent being distributed through freestanding inserts (FSI). FSI are sheets of coupons distributed in newspapers, primarily on Sunday. Another 4 percent of coupons are distributed through direct mail and 3.5 percent more are distributed either in or on a product's package. The remaining 5 percent are delivered in other ways.[8]

CREATIVE

Creatives are the individuals who develop advertising and promotional messages and campaigns. Most creatives are employed by advertising agencies, but some work within individual companies or as freelancers. Creatives usually have backgrounds in art, graphic design, production, theater, or journalism.

The creative works with the advertising agency executive and the client company to develop specific advertisements or to design an advertising campaign. Guided by a creative brief, the creative looks for innovative, entertaining, and attention-getting methods for capturing the consumer's attention and reaching other marketing goals.

CREATIVE BRIEF

In preparing advertisements and advertising campaigns, creatives work with a document called a creative strategy or creative brief. A creative brief helps the creative to incorporate all of the information provided by the account executive and the client to produce advertisements. The goal of a creative brief is to guide the process so that the final advertisement conveys the desired message in a manner that will have a positive impact on potential customers. The components of a creative brief are

- the objective,
- the target audience,

- the message theme,
- the support, and
- the constraints.

The objective of the advertisement guides the entire process of ad creation. Typical objectives include increasing brand awareness, building brand image, generating customer traffic, providing information, and increasing orders. The target audience is the set of consumers, or market segment, being targeted by a particular advertisement. This is usually a subset of the product's target market. For example, a product may be targeted to females ages fifteen to fifty, but the ad being designed may target only fifteen- to twenty-four-year-old females. A message theme is an outline of key ideas that the advertisement is supposed to convey. For a milk advertisement, a key message theme could be to convey that milk contains calcium, which prevents bone loss as women grow older. The support is any documentation or study that will support the message theme. A study by the American Medical Association can be used to show that calcium prevents osteoporosis in women. The constraints are any legal or mandatory restrictions that must be placed on an advertisement. These include legal protection for trademarks, logos, and copy registrations.

CULTURAL SYMBOL POSITIONING STRATEGY

Positioning is the process of creating a perception in the minds of consumers concerning the nature of a brand relative to the competition. Possible positioning approaches include attributes, competitors, use or application, price-quality, product user, product class, and cultural symbol.

Helping a product or company become a cultural symbol is difficult. When successful, a strong competitive advantage emerges. One well-known example of a cultural positioning strategy has been the image-building efforts of Chevrolet. During the summer, the company often advertises that Chevrolet is as American as baseball and apple pie. Playboy has evolved into an entertainment empire by becoming a cultural symbol, albeit a controversial one. Stetson advertisements identify the cologne with cultural symbols such as an American cowboy and the spirit of the West, in a manner similar to the campaigns featuring the Marlboro Man in the late 1900s.

CUSTOMER ANALYSIS

A customer analysis is part of a communications market analysis. After a target market has been identified by the process, the next step is to conduct a customer analysis. Three types of customers are studied:

1. Current company customers
2. The competition's customers
3. Potential customers who currently do not purchase from a particular company but may become interested

The goal of customer analyses is to reveal their interpretations of the organization's advertisements and other marketing communications. The point is to find out what works within each customer base. It is helpful to ascertain how customers perceive individual advertisements as well as what they think about the larger company.

CYBERBAIT

Cyberbait is a special type of financial incentive offered over the Internet to lure or attract people to a Web site. Cyberbait includes special offers such as loss-leader products, unusual items that cannot be purchased elsewhere, or other incentives. Some Internet companies provide games that consumers can play to bring them to a site. Others offer daily or weekly tips on various topics to entice return visits. For example, for a business-to-business health site, a weekly tip on how to reduce health risks and job-related injuries may be a cyberbait that attracts prospects to the site. To entice consumers and businesses to return to the site on a regular basis, additional cyberbait is needed. E-shoppers routinely surf the Net and search competing sites. Therefore, these individuals need a reason to return to a particular site on a regular basis. Cyberbait is one method companies use to achieve return traffic.

DAY-AFTER RECALL

One key goal of many marketing communication and advertising programs is consumer recall. If individuals do not remember an advertisement, it is not effective. The most common method for evaluating recall is the day-after recall (DAR) test. The DAR method is used to evaluate television, radio, magazine, and newspaper advertisements, with television advertisements making the most frequent use of DAR.

Individuals who participate in a DAR test receive phone calls the day after the advertisement first appears. Normally, they are tested using an unaided recall method in which the subjects are asked to name, or recall, the ads they saw or heard the previous evening, without being given any prompts or memory jogs. Two approaches may be used for magazines and newspapers. In the first, consumers are contacted the day after the ad appeared. The individuals name the ads they recall and then are asked a series of questions to see if they remember features of the advertisement. In the second, an individual is given a magazine for a certain period of time (normally one week) and instructed to read it as he or she normally would during leisure time. Then the researcher returns and asks a series of questions about which ads were memorable and what features the individual could remember. In the business-to-business sector, the second method is a popular way to test ads for trade journals.

DAR is a valuable tool for advertisers because increased recall enhances the probability that the brand will become a part of the consumer's evoked set. The evoked set is a set of brand options that are remembered when purchase alternatives are being considered and would be considered viable choices. (*See* EVOKED SET *for additional information.*)

DECAY EFFECTS

Decay effects occur after advertising for a company or brand has been stopped. Soon the consumers or businesses that were exposed to the ads begin to forget them. In some cases, decay effects are rapid, while in others the process is long and slow. The rate of decay is dependent upon many factors, but two of the most important are the strength of the brand's image and the intensity of the advertising program that was discontinued. Brands with strong images and brands that were advertised intensively will experience slower decay effects. Also, some advertisements are more memorable than others, due to the use of humor or some other technique. These ads would also experience slower decay effects. (*See* CARRYOVER EFFECTS; SALES-RESPONSE FUNCTION CURVE; *and* THRESHOLD EFFECT *for additional information.*)

DECEPTIVE AND MISLEADING ADVERTISEMENTS

One frequent criticism of advertising is that it is deceptive and misleading. It is clear that some companies and marketing firms are guilty of this offense, but the U.S. government has in place laws and regulatory agencies that prevent or stop such practices. Most notably, the Federal Trade Commission works to stop companies from preparing deceptive and misleading advertisements.

Although consumers may doubt the truthfulness of ads, members of the advertising profession note that deceptive and misleading ads are rare. Deceitful advertisements are not in the best interests of a firm, because they cause long-term damage to the firm's image. Customers who believe they have been cheated will not return. Also, negative publicity and bad word-of-mouth can force a firm out of business. Thus, the free market system normally punishes firms that consistently use deceptive advertising. Governmental regulators also do their part. Lawsuits against offending companies tend to further discourage such unethical practices. (*See* FEDERAL TRADE COMMISSION *for additional information.*)

DECIDER

A decider is a member of a business buying center. Deciders are the individuals who authorize purchase decisions. In most companies, purchase decisions for high-cost items are made by a financial officer, a vice president, or even the president. For lower-cost items, the decider may be a purchasing agent or even the person who uses the product. Normally the decider is an officer or administrative official in the company with the authority to approve purchases.

DECODING

Decoding is the process of interpreting an advertising message. Decoding takes place as the receiver employs any set of his or her senses (hearing, seeing, feeling, etc.) to capture and interpret a message. Most messages reach more than one sense. In a conversation, the people involved both see and hear each other. They may also touch and feel during the same conversation.

In the area of advertising, decoding occurs as consumers encounter messages in various ways. They hear and see television ads. Coupons are touched and seen as the consumer reads a coupon offer. It is even possible to smell a message. A well-placed perfume sample may entice a buyer to purchase both the magazine containing the sample and the perfume being advertised.

DECORATIVE MODEL

Decorative models are defined as models in an advertisement whose primary purpose is to adorn the product as a sexual or attractive stimulus. The person serves no purpose other than to attract attention to the advertisement. Automobile, tool, and beer companies have often utilized female models dressed in bikinis to stand by products. The basic conclusions of studies that have examined the impact of decorative models are as follows:

- The presence of female (or male) decorative models improves ad recognition, but not brand recognition.
- The presence of a decorative model influences emotional and objective evaluations of the product among both male and female audiences.

- Attractive models produce a higher level of attention to ads than do less attractive models.
- The presence of an attractive model produces stronger purchase intentions when the product is sexually relevant than if it is not sexually relevant.

Increasingly, women's groups and other social critics have attacked the use of decorative models in advertising and marketing programs, and as a result the use of decorative models has decreased in recent years.

DEMOGRAPHICS

Demographics are population characteristics. These characteristics can be used to identity consumer groups and target markets. In advertising, typical demographic segmentation variables include gender, age, education, income, race, and/or ethnicity. Using demographics to identify market segments is based on the idea that people with distinguishable demographic characteristics have common needs that may be different than needs of other groups. Consequently, many goods and services are created to meet the needs of individual demographic segments. Then advertising messages are tailored to those specific groups.

DEMONSTRATION EXECUTION

Demonstration execution is a type of executional framework. Other types of executional frameworks include animation, slice-of-life, dramatization, testimonials, authoritative, fantasy, and informative. A demonstration executional framework is designed to show how a product works. Such a demonstration is an effective way to communicate the attributes and use of a product to customers and others. This is because the product's benefits can be described as the product is being exhibited and used.

A demonstration execution can be used, for example, to display a new form of dust cloth that can be attached to a handle or used separately. The demonstration would highlight the product's multiple uses by cleaning a television screen, a table, and a saxophone, and, with the handle attached, by reaching a light fixture on the ceiling. Thus, consumers are shown how to use the product and can observe its advantages at the same time.

Demonstrations are often present in business-to-business advertisements and marketing messages. They allow a business to show how a product can meet the specific needs of another business. The Amway Company relies heavily on demonstrations to entice retail customers to buy products and to convince individuals to begin selling their merchandise. By also using magazine and brochure ads the firm is able to attract both types of customers.

Demonstration-type ads routinely appear on television. To a limited extent, print media can feature demonstrations, especially when a series of photos shows the sequence of product usage.

DERIVED DEMAND

Derived demand is based on, linked to, or derived from the production and sale of some other consumer good or service. For example, the demand for steel is based largely on the number of cars and trucks sold each year. When the demand for vehicles goes down because the economy experiences a recession or downturn, the demand for steel also declines. For steel manufacturers, it is difficult to stimulate demand because of the nature of derived demand. Derived demand is often associated with the raw materials that are used in the production of goods and services, such as steel, aluminum, concrete, plastic, petroleum products (e.g., jet fuel for airlines), construction materials, and so forth. Derived demand also exists for services. For example, demand for mortgage loans is directly dependent on housing sales.

DIRECT MARKETING

When a manufacturer sells directly to end users, the company is employing a direct marketing program. Direct marketing makes it possible to develop closer relationships with customers. They can enhance loyalty to a brand or company rather than to a retailer. Direct marketing programs often generate greater profits since the middle channel members are bypassed. The most typical media channels for direct marketing include

- mail,
- catalogs,
- telemarketing,
- mass media,
- alternative media, and
- Internet and e-mail.

Historically, the most common form of direct marketing was through the mail. Mail remains an effective direct marketing tool in many situations. Such programs can generate leads and also obtain orders. The impact of direct mail is easily measurable by comparing the number mailed to the number of responses and sales. Direct mail can be easily targeted to various consumer groups. Marketing teams can test every component of a direct mail campaign, including the type of offer, the copy in the ad, graphics used, color, and the size of the direct mail packet. Some consumers object, however, to "junk mail."

Many consumers respond more favorably to catalogs, which can be viewed at one's leisure. Catalogs provide low-pressure offers to consumers who already have some interest in the product or company. Many specialty goods are sold through catalog orders.

Telemarketing is another tool used for direct marketing. Database information makes it possible for callers to contact the best prospects in order to sell merchandise. Recent "no call" legislation has made telemarketing more difficult. At the same time, inbound telemarketing can be an important component of a direct marketing campaign. Taking inbound calls helps support messages provided in advertisements. Consequently, toll-free numbers are often prominently and frequently displayed in all direct marketing and advertising materials to make sure consumers know where to go to gather additional information and place orders.

Mass media are often part of a direct marketing campaign. The most common forms of mass media used in direct marketing are television, radio, magazines, and newspapers. Television delivers access to a mass audience. For products with a more general appeal to the masses, network television is an excellent medium to reach many consumers with a single message. Again, an ad normally includes a toll-free number and a Web site so that consumers can quickly place orders. They may also request further information and ask questions about the product or company. Radio does not have the reach of television but still can be used to convey strong messages. Toll-free numbers and Web addresses stated in radio ads must be easy to remember and repeated frequently, because consumers may not have the opportunity to write them down.

Print media (newspapers and magazines) are also used for direct marketing. They can be utilized to target specific audiences. They make it possible to offer detailed information to key potential customers. Print ads highlight toll-free numbers and Web site addresses for consumers, so that they are easy to see.

The Internet provides a new and popular channel for direct marketing. For most companies, the Internet is a place for consumers and businesses to get more information. For many, using the Internet is less intrusive than calling a toll-free number. Once on the Internet, many consumers are willing to place orders. Many companies use the Internet to display goods and services customers can order directly. In addition to Web site Internet programs, many companies are developing e-mail direct marketing campaigns. E-mail makes it possible for the company to deliver customized messages or promotions.

DRAMATIZATION EXECUTION

Dramatization is a type of executional framework. Other types of executional frameworks include animation, slice-of-life, testimonials, authoritative, demonstration, fantasy, and informative. A dramatization is similar to a slice-of-life executional framework in that it uses the same format of presenting a problem then providing a solution through the following four steps:

1. Encounter
2. Problem
3. Interaction
4. Solution

The difference between a dramatization and a slice-of-life execution lies in the intensity and story format. Dramatization uses a higher level of excitement and suspense to tell the story. A dramatization story normally builds to a crisis point.

An effective dramatic advertisement is difficult to create. The entire drama must play out in either thirty or sixty seconds. Building a story to a climatic moment is challenging, given such a short time period. Consequently, not all dramatic executional styles accomplish the high level of suspense that is required to make them successful. Creatives must find ways to tell the story quickly to achieve the desired effects.

DUAL-CHANNEL MARKETING

Dual-channel marketing takes place when firms sell virtually the same goods or services to both consumers and businesses. The most common form occurs when a product is first sold in business markets and then is adapted to consumer markets. New products often have high start-up costs, including R&D expenditures and market research. Businesses tend to be less price sensitive than retail consumers thus it is logical to sell to them first.

Economies of scale emerge as sales increase. This leads to larger purchases of raw materials combined with more standardized methods of production, which in turn makes it possible to enter consumer markets. These economies of scale entice manufacturers to sell products previously supplied to the business sector in the retail markets. Products such as digital cameras, calculators, computers, fax machines, and cellular phones were first marketed to businesses and then later to consumers.

To move a product from the business market to consumers normally requires that prices come down and products become more user friendly. For example, consumers can now place photos on a CD rather than obtaining traditional prints. The imaging technology that was developed by Kodak and Intel and first sold to various businesses has become more user friendly and cheaper, thereby allowing it to be sold through the retail channel.

EFFECTIVE FREQUENCY AND EFFECTIVE REACH

Effective frequency is the number of exposures receives an audience from a particular message designed to achieve a specific objective. Effective reach is the percentage of an audience that must be exposed to a particular message to achieve a specific objective. Implied in the concepts of effective frequency and effective reach is that some minimum number of exposures is needed to accomplish a marketing or advertising objective.

Advertisers are acutely aware of the importance of effective frequency and effective reach. Too few exposures means the advertiser fails to attain its intended objectives, because consumers do not recall advertisements. On the other hand, too many exposures waste resources if the additional exposures have no additional impact. The goal is to identify the optimal reach and frequency mix to accomplish the intended objectives without experiencing diminishing returns from extra ads. An additional challenge appears when consumer differences are considered. It may take three exposures to an advertisement to impact one consumer while it takes ten for another. Differences in the ages of customers, their interests, personalities, and media preferences all influence recall and therefore require different levels of effective reach and frequency.

ELABORATION LIKELIHOOD MODEL

The elaboration likelihood models (ELM) is an information processing model. It is based on the idea that individuals will take the time to consider persuasive communication messages that are designed to change consumer attitudes. Information processing occurs through two routes in the ELM model. The first is the central processing route. When a consumer cognitively processes a message giving a high degree of attention to the major or core elements of that message, then the pathway is the central processing route. For example, the core message that a wireless telephone has a clear, consistent signal should affect attitudes that are adopted through the central route, in this case the belief that the provider has a superior service. If the consumer adopts that attitude it will be more firmly held, longer-lasting, and resistant to change. Furthermore, attitudes that emerge based on frequent exposures to advertisements are excellent predictors of subsequent behaviors. Consequently, a young man or woman who has developed the attitude that Marines are indeed "the few, the proud" is more likely to enlist as a young adult.

The peripheral route is an alternate route for processing information. This second path is followed when viewers pay attention to the more marginal cues embedded in a communication message. In a television advertisement, peripheral cues include music, actors, and the background (beach, mountains, and forests). An antacid which is supposed to soothe the stomach is likely to be presented with peripheral cues such as a calm voice-over, a blue background, and soothing music.

Consumers using the peripheral route pay less attention to the primary message or argument. Instead, they focus on one or more peripheral cues. A favorable or negative attitude will develop based on these peripheral cues. A negative attitude may emerge if the endorser is disliked. The dislike transfers from the endorser to the product, and the viewer may not have even listened to or considered what was said during the commercial. Attitudes formed by the peripheral route tend to be less rigid, and less resistant to change. They are poorer predictors of subsequent behaviors than messages processed through the central route.

The route chosen by consumers is determined by two factors: motivation and ability. Motivation affects the willingness to engage in information search and the manner in which the information is processed. A motivated individual searches for more information and has a greater tendency to process the information using the central route. Highly motivated consumers pay closer attention to the core message argument of an advertisement than they do to peripheral cues.

The second factor, ability, is a consumer's intrinsic desire to use his or her cognitive skills. Individuals who enjoy thinking tend to cognitively process more of the elements of the environment around them.

They will pay more attention to the primary message arguments in advertisements and are also more inclined to use the central route.

To reach the peripheral path, repetition is an effective technique. The more often a consumer sees a particular advertisement, the better the chances that a message argument will be processed. Then a greater number of exposures to the same advertisement or communication normally causes the peripheral cues to become less important as customers pay more attention to the core message. The ELM assumes consumers make rational purchase decisions. Clearly, however, not all purchase decisions are rational. (*See* HEDONIC EXPERIENTIAL MODEL *for another approach to information processing.*)

ENCODING PROCESS

Encoding is a component of the communication process. Forming verbal (words, sounds) and nonverbal (gestures, facial expression, posture) cues is the encoding step, in which the sender creates and dispatches a message. Encoding is a key ingredient in the communication process related to the marketing of goods and services. The goal is to capture the attention of anyone who is planning to buy an item. The advertising creative will look for ways to encode marketing ideas in forms that capture the viewer's attention. In the advertisements several verbal and nonverbal tactics will be used. Attractive spokespersons, familiar music, and visually exciting images are often part of effectively utilizing the encoding process.

EMOTIONAL APPEAL

An emotional appeal is a tactic in which a product, brand, or company is connected to emotions, such as love, friendship, patriotism, fear, and security. Emotional appeals are based on three issues. The first is that consumers ignore most advertisements. Second, rational advertising appeals may not be noticed unless the consumer is in the market for a particular product. Third, instead of rational methods, emotional advertising can capture a viewer's attention and help develop an attachment between the consumer and a brand.

Emotional advertising is one method to develop brand loyalty. The idea is to cause customers to bond with a brand. Emotional appeals reach the more creative right side of the brain; therefore visual cues are important in emotional appeals. A common advertising tactic is to combine humor with emotions. Another is to focus on the consumer's life and feelings.

Recently, many business-to-business advertisers have begun using emotional appeals. The rationale is that emotions affect all types of purchase decisions. Members of the buying center study product information in making decisions but at the same time can be affected by the same emotions as regular consumers. Although members of the buying center may try to minimize the emotional side of a purchase, many are still affected by emotions. In the past, only 5 to 10 percent of all business-to-business ads utilized emotional appeals. Now the percentage is around 25 percent.

Television is an ideal medium for emotional appeals. It offers intrusion value and has both sound and visual images. Facial expressions can convey emotions and attitudes. Consumers may learn, vicariously, about a particular product and develop an attitude based on these vicarious experiences. Television ads are vivid and lifelike. They can feature dynamic situations designed to pull the viewer into the ad. Music makes the ad even more dramatic. Such peripheral cues (music, background visuals, etc.) are important components of emotional appeals because they attract the attention of a viewer. (*See* ELABORATION LIKELIHOOD MODEL *for additional information.*)

EMOTIONAL MESSAGE STRATEGY

A message strategy is the primary tactic used in the creation of an advertising message. Message strategies can be divided into four categories: cognitive, affective, conative, and brand. The affective message strategies, in turn, can be divided into the two subcategories of resonance and emotional.

An emotional strategy is an attempt to elicit powerful emotions in an advertisement that enhance product recall and brand choice. Many emotions can be connected to products, including trust, reliability, friendship, happiness, security, glamour, luxury, serenity, pleasure, romance, and passion. Emotional message strategies are used mostly in consumer advertisements. However, emotional appeals in business-to-business ads are increasing because members of the buying center are human beings who do not always make decisions based on only rational thought processes. Emotions and feelings can affect decisions. If the product's benefits can be presented within an emotional framework, the advertisement is normally more effective.

EMOTIONAL REACTION TEST

Many ads are designed to elicit emotional responses from consumers. Emotional ads are designed to cause positive emotions that are more likely to be remembered. Consumers who develop positive attitudes toward ads would logically have more positive attitudes toward the product. This, in turn, should result in increased purchases.[9]

Many approaches are used to measure the emotional impact of an advertisement. The simplest method is to ask questions about an individual's feelings and emotions after viewing an ad. This can be performed in a laboratory-setting theater test or the ad can be shown to a focus group. In both circumstances, the test ad should placed with other ads.

A warmth monitor is a second method to measure emotions. Feelings of warmth may be directed toward an ad or a product. To measure warmth, subjects manipulate a joystick while watching a commercial. The movements track reactions to a commercial by making marks on a sheet of paper containing four lines labeled as follows:

1. Absence of warmth
2. Neutral
3. Warmhearted/tender
4. Emotional

Although the warmth meter was developed to evaluate television ads, it can also be used for radio advertising. New versions have even been developed for the Internet.

Most of the time, emotions are associated with shorter term events, such as the reaction to a given advertisement. At the same time, emotions are strongly held in the memory of most consumers. Therefore, an ad that made a viewer angry may be retrieved and the anger re-cre-ated every time the individual remembers either the ad or the company. As a result, it is wise to attempt to discover emotional responses to various ads before they are shown to the general public.

EVALUATION OF ALTERNATIVES (PURCHASING DECISION PROCESS)

The third step in the decision-making process is the evaluation of alternatives. During this stage consumers evaluate the various purchase possibilities. Three models have been formulated to explain the process of evaluation:

1. Evoked set
2. Multiattribute
3. Affect referral

Consumers may use thought processes that resemble one or more of these models during the evaluation of alternatives. The method depends on the circumstances of the purchase situation and the consumer's previous experiences. The evoked set approach implies that a consumer utilizes internal search for information. An evoked set consists of the feasible products and brands that come to mind that can effectively meet the consumer's need. These choices are in the "top of mind" category, or the first ones that come to mind.

The multiattribute model requires more deliberation. Such a thinking process includes an external search for additional data. The consumer evaluates each alternative along various attributes, choosing the brand that provides the highest overall score or global rating. For example, when choosing a new television set, the consumer may consider the price, size, clarity of picture, and service contract, giving each a "weight" or rating. The set with the best combination of features is the one that is most likely to be chosen.

Affect referral is a thought process in which the consumer relies on the brand or the product that he or she believes will best meet a need. The top choice is the one about which the individual has the strongest and most positive feelings. Brand loyalty is closely related to an affect referral type of approach for evaluating purchasing possibilities.

(*See* AFFECT REFERRAL; EVOKED SET; *and* MULTIATTRIBUTE AP-PROACH *for additional information.*)

EVALUATION CRITERIA FOR ADVERTISEMENTS

A useful methodology in developing criteria to evaluate advertising is called PACT, or positioning advertising copytesting. PACT was developed by twenty-one leading U.S. advertising agencies to evaluate television ads.[10] Although the original intention for PACT was to examine copytesting for television ads, the principles can be used for any type of advertising evaluation and all types of media.

The first principle of PACT is that regardless of the evaluation technique used, the evaluation method should be relevant to the advertising objective being tested. For example, if the objective of a price-off promotion is to stimulate additional sales, then the test should evaluate the display of the price-off offer to determine its ability to stimulate additional sales. On the other hand, an evaluation of consumer attitudes toward brands requires a different instrument.

The second PACT principle is that researchers should agree on how results will be used when selecting test instruments. They should also agree on the design of the test. This is especially true for the preparation stage in an advertisement's development. A variety of tests can be used to determine whether or not an advertisement will eventually be completed.

Third, a cutoff score should be set for a test prior to administering the test. The cutoff score is designed to prevent biases from entering evaluations of an ad's potential effectiveness. Many ad agencies use test markets for new advertisements before they are launched in a larger area. When a recall method is used to determine if people in the target market remember seeing the ad, a prearranged cutoff score should be in place. For instance, the requirement may be that 25 percent of consumers in the test market area should remember the ad before the campaign can move forward. If the percentage is not reached, the ad has failed the test.

Fourth, PACT suggests that using multiple measures will allow more precise evaluations of ads and campaigns. This is because many times an ad may fail one particular testing procedure yet score higher on others. Consumers and business buyers who are the targets of advertising communications are complex human beings with varying perceptions of advertisements. The PACT method suggests that it is helpful to develop more than one measure to achieve greater agreement on whether or not an ad or campaign will succeed and reach its desired goals.

A test to evaluate an advertisement should be based on some theory or model of human response to communication, which is the fifth PACT principle. A theory-based test is more likely to accurately predict human behavior. Since the objective is to enhance the odds that the communication will actually produce the desired results (going to the Web site, visiting the store, making a purchase, etc.), theory-based tests are superior.

Many testing procedures are based on a single exposure. The sixth PACT principle states that although in many cases a single exposure is sufficient for research purposes, it is more likely that multiple exposures are needed to obtain reliable test results. More than one exposure is often required when the message is complex, since the human mind is able to comprehend only so much information in one viewing. It is vital to make sure the person can and does comprehend the ad to determine whether the ad can achieve its desired effects.

Placing the test advertisement with others means the test subjects do not know which ad is being evaluated. This prevents personal biases from affecting judgments. To ensure valid results, the alternative ads should be in the same stage of process development, which is the seventh PACT principle.

Eight, advertising teams should be certain that adequate controls are in place to prevent biases and other external factors from affecting results. One method is to use an experimental design to control external factors. This helps researchers to keep as many things (control variables) as constant as possible while manipulating only one variable at a time. Thus, in a theater test, the temperature, time of day, room lighting, television program, and ads shown can all be the same, making them control variables. Then the researcher may display the program and ads to an all-male audience followed by an all-female audience. Changing only one variable (gender) makes it possible to study the ad in a controlled environment to find out if it was perceived differently by men than by women. At that same time, field tests can also be effective. Testing advertisements in real-world situations is valuable, because the goal is often to approximate reality. When conducting a field test, such as a mall intercept, those performing the test will try to control as many variables as possible. Thus, the same mall, same questions, and same ads are used. Then age, gender, or other variables can be manipulated.

PACT principle nine is that a sample being used to test an advertisement should be representative of the target population. As with any research procedure, sampling procedures are important. Consequently, a print ad designed for Hispanic Americans should be tested using a sample of Spanish-American or Hispanic consumers.

Finally, researchers must continually seek to make tests reliable and valid. Reliable means repeatable. In other words, if the same test is given five times to the same person, the individual should respond in the same way each time. If a respondent picks "emotional" on one iteration of a warmth test and "neutral" when the ad is shown a second time, the research team will begin to wonder if the test is reliable.

Valid means generalizable. Valid research findings can be generalized to other groups. For instance, when a focus group of women finds an ad to be funny, and then a group of men reacts in the same way, the finding that the humor is effective is more valid. This would be an increasingly valuable outcome if the results were generalizable to people of various ages and races. Many times an ad may be reliable or repeatable in the same group, but not valid or generalizable to other groups of consumers or business buyers. (*See also* POSITIONING ADVERTISING COPYTESTING.)

EVENT MARKETING

Event marketing occurs when a company supports a specific event. It is similar to sponsorship marketing. A sponsorship involves a person, group, or team, while event marketing is targeted at an event. Most event marketing activities includes setting up a booth or display and having some type of physical presence at the event. Almost $8 billion is spent annually on event marketing. General Motors and Philip Morris have been the top two event marketing spenders in the past.[11]

Many events are sports related. Rodeos and music concerts often become marketing events. In addition, many more segmented events are held. For instance, a Hispanic fiesta funded by a food company is a targeted event. A health fair conducted by a local hospital (e.g., An Affair of the Heart wellness program) is another form of event marketing.

The goal of event marketing is to achieve brand name recognition. These programs can also help a manufacturer develop closer ties with vendors and customers. Furthermore, events can boost morale for the employees who participate or attend. Sponsoring local events provides a company with the potential to generate free publicity. These events may also enhance the company's image in the local community. Several key steps are required when preparing an event. Therefore, to ensure the maximum benefit from event sponsorships, companies should do the following:[12]

1. Determine the objectives of sponsoring events.
2. Match each event with customers, vendors, or employees.
3. Cross-promote the event.
4. Make sure the company is included in all of the event's advertising and brochures.
5. Track results.
6. Evaluate the investment following the event.

It is crucial to match the event with a segment or target market. Sponsoring participants at an event normally insist on placement of the company name, logo, and other product information in every advertisement and brochure. Attendees of special events often keep programs as souvenirs to show others. Placing the sponsor's name and message on the program generates an ad with a long life span. The sponsoring business must work to maximize brand name exposure by connecting the firm's name with the event's marketing program. The event management team should make sure that the sponsor's name receives prominent attention in all materials associated with the event.

EVOKED SET

An evoked set is used when a consumer is conducting an internal search of purchasing alternatives. The evoked set consists of the brands the individual considers. The set does not normally contain every brand the consumer has experienced. Brands that have been tried with negative results are removed from the evoked set. Also, brands that the consumer knows little about are usually eliminated. The evoked set helps the consumer reduce the number of brands to be considered to a subset that he or she can mentally manage.

Creatives, advertising executives, and brand managers work to make sure a given brand becomes part of the majority of consumer evoked sets. Brands that are part of the evoked set are much more likely to be purchased. Attractive and powerful advertising messages greatly enhance the odds that a good or service will be remembered and considered as a finalist in a purchasing decision.

Two additional components of evoked sets are part of the evaluation of purchase alternatives: the inept set and the inert set. An inept set holds the brands that are part of a person's memory that will not be considered because they elicit negative feelings. These negative sentiments are normally caused by a bad experience with a vendor or particular brand. An inept set may also hold brands that have received negative comments from a friend or acquaintance or because the consumer has seen an advertisement that he or she did not like.

The inert set consists of brands that the consumer is aware of but with no corresponding negative or positive feelings about the products. In a cognitive map, these brands have not entered any individual map, or they have only weak linkages to other ideas. The lack of knowledge about these brands usually eliminates them as alternatives. This is because in most purchase situations the only brands that are considered are those that are strongly present in the evoked set. (*See* AFFECT REFERRAL *and* MULTIATTRIBUTE MODEL *for additional methods of evaluating purchase alternatives.*)

EXECUTIONAL FRAMEWORK

The manner in which an advertising appeal is presented is an executional framework. An ad appeal is similar to a script for a movie (e.g., comedy, drama, action film). The plot of the movie is the executional framework. The creative chooses an executional framework while working with the media buyer and the account executive. The most common advertising executions include

- animation,
- slice-of-life,
- dramatization,
- testimonial,
- authoritative,
- demonstration,
- fantasy, and
- informative.

Animation is the use of cartoon characters, personifications, or hand- or computer-generated characters. The slice-of-life execution involves portraying the product within a typical life situation. Dramatization is similar to the slice-of-life except that the plot is more dramatic. Testimonials involve the use of paid endorsers or customers providing testimonies about a product. An authoritative execution utilizes some type of authority figure or organization to substantiate claims. With the demonstration approach, advertisers show or illustrate how the product performs or is used. The fantasy execution uses an element of make-believe or imagination in the advertisement, and the informative execution involves providing information in a straightforward manner. *(For more information about executional frameworks, see each of the ad executions listed above.)*

EXPERT AUTHORITY

Expertise is utilized in advertising when the advertisement seeks to convince consumers that a product is superior to other brands. The ad will feature the use of an expert or authority. The expert or authority may be a doctor, lawyer, scientist, or an individual having more specific knowledge, such as an athlete who endorses a product that relieves muscle pain and helps the athlete win an event. Expert authority also emerges from quoting research statistics. Noting that *Consumer Reports* magazine rates a product highly is another form of expert endorsement.

EXTERNAL SEARCH

A search for information is the second step in the consumer decision-making process. As a consumer looks for a solution to a need or want that arises, the first search is internal. The second search is external. If the customer has sufficient information internally, then he or she will not conduct an external search but will simply move to the next stage of the decision-making process, which is the evaluation of alternatives. When the consumer feels uncertain about the right brand to purchase, then an external search takes place.

External information can be gathered from a variety of sources. Friends, relatives, expert consumers, books, magazines, newspapers, advertisements, public relations stories, in-store displays, salespeople, and Internet searches can all become part of an external search.

The amount of time a consumer will spend on an external search depends on four factors: (1) ability, (2) motivation, (3) costs, and (4) benefits. The four factors are normally considered at the same time. Thus, when the perceived cost of a search is low and the perceived benefit is high, the consumer is motivated to search for information. A consumer with a minimal amount of product knowledge and a low level of education is less likely to undertake an external search because the consumer lacks the ability to find the right information. The motivation to conduct an external search will also be affected by the type of product being considered as well as the purchase situation. For instance, when buying a watch for personal use, the person may do little external searching. At the same time, buying a watch for a significant other may cause the person to be highly motivated to conduct a thorough external search to ensure that a wise purchase is made.

FAMILY BRAND

A family brand is one in which a company offers a series or group of products under one brand name. Family brands are found in a variety of products, including automobiles, insurance, food, power tools, and numerous others. A family brand is used to tie the image of the brand name to every new product that is added to a current line. Transfer associations occur when the new product is within the same product category. However, if additional products are added that are not related to the brand's core merchandise, the transfer of loyalty becomes more difficult.

FAMILY LIFE CYCLE

The family life cycle is a method to portray how consumers change as they age. At each stage in the cycle, different challenges or interests are present. Consequently, consumer purchasing behavior is affected by the stages of the family life cycle. The standard stages in the life cycle of the family include

- being single (bachelorhood),
- newlyweds with no children,
- first families (with young children),
- full nest (with growing and teenage children),
- empty nest (children have moved out), and
- remaining partner (following death of a spouse).

Each of these stages creates unique marketing opportunities and each places a different priority on purchases. Single people tend to seek out excitement, romance, and independence. Newlyweds are adjusting to a new living pattern and are looking for household items to help them settle into a home. First families often center attention on small children, making clothes purchases and school items most important. A full nest is characterized by numerous time demands and the desire for convenience. Empty nest families think more about retirement and a more leisurely pace of life. Remaining partners are often acutely aware of estates and other issues related to inheritance.

FANTASY EXECUTION

A fantasy approach is a type of executional framework. Other types of executional frameworks include animation, slice-of-life, dramatization, testimonials, authoritative, demonstration, and informative. Fantasy executions lift the audience beyond the real world using a make-believe experience. Some fantasies are portrayed in a fairly realistic manner, whereas others are designed to be completely irrational. Irrational and illogical ads are often more clearly remembered by an audience. A fantasy execution can be used in a variety of settings for many different types of products.

The most common fantasy themes deal with sex, love, and romance. According to some marketing experts, raw sex and nudity in advertisements are losing their impact. Advertisers can use a fantasy execution that can be designed to fit with preferences for a tamer sexuality. Many senior citizens and older individuals find raw sex and nudity to be offensive. Fantasy is an excellent way to approach them by creating a world of romantic make-believe rather than hard-driving sexuality.[13]

A product category that often uses the fantasy execution is the perfume and cologne. Currently, perfume and cologne advertisers portray products as something that will enhance a couple's love life. They also can show the product as a way to make a man or woman feel more sensuous.

Television fantasy ads for cruise lines show couples enjoying romantic, sensuous vacations together, swimming, Jet Skiing, and spending time together. The goal is to make the cruise into more than just a vacation—it should become a romantic fantasy trip. Fantasy ads can also show people experiencing the thrill of winning a major sports event or sharing a common product (beer, pizza) with a beautiful model. An effective fantasy execution assists in recall and leads to a consumer action, such as visiting a store or making a purchase.

FEAR APPEAL

A fear appeal is designed to use consumer fears to inspire purchases. Consumers may fear a variety of negative circumstances, such as ill health, death, financial problems, social rejection, and poverty. Consequently, advertisers use fear to sell a variety of products. Life insurance companies focus on the consequences of not having life insurance if a person dies. Shampoo and mouthwash ads invoke fears of dandruff and bad breath, since they can make a person a social outcast.[14] The design of a fear appeal is normally based on showing negative consequences that occur when a particular action is taken or when a particular brand is not purchased.

Research indicates that a fear appeal increases viewer interest in an advertisement as well as the persuasiveness of an ad. Consumers who pay more attention to an advertisement are more likely to process the information and recall it at a later time. Many individuals remember advertisements with fear appeals better than they do warm, upbeat messages.

Two components of fear that are of interest in advertisements are severity and vulnerability. Severity is the degree of consequences that are possible. An extremely severe consequence would be injury or death. A mild level of severity might be embarrassment. Vulnerability refers to the likelihood or probability that the negative consequence will occur. As an example, a business-to-business advertiser could use fear to promote an e-commerce platform. Severity is reflected in the consequences of downtime when an e-commerce platform crashes. Vulnerability is displayed by showing the probability that an e-commerce platform can crash.

A difficult decision in fear advertising is the strength of the appeal. Typically, a moderate level of fear is the most effective. Low levels of fear are less likely to be noticed, and the fear level may not be convincing in terms of severity or vulnerability. Fear levels that are too high may be detrimental, because the message creates feelings of anxiety. This leads viewers to avoid watching the ad by changing the channel or muting the sound.[15] A fear ad should be strong enough to attract viewer attention and to influence, but not so strong that the person avoids seeing the advertisement.

FEDERAL COMMUNICATIONS COMMISSION

A primary regulatory agency associated with advertising and marketing communications is the Federal Communications Commission (FCC). The FCC has authority over the television, radio, and telephone industries. The FCC both grants and revokes operating licenses for radio and television stations. Consumer complaints about programming may be registered with the FCC. The FCC also specifies ownership limits, such as how many stations in one marketplace can be owned by a single individual or company. Congress may vote to overrule any FCC decision regarding ownership percentages, as occurred in 2003.

The FCC does not have authority over the content of advertisements transmitted by mass media. Furthermore, the FCC does not control which products may or may not be advertised. The FCC is, however, charged with the responsibility of monitoring advertising directed to children. Current FCC rules state that television stations must limit children's advertisements to twelve minutes per hour during weekdays and ten and one half minutes per hour on weekends.

FEDERAL TRADE COMMISSION

The Federal Trade Commission (FTC) is the federal agency that has the most direct jurisdiction over advertising and marketing communications as well as over any practice that prohibits or restricts free trade. The FTC was created in 1914 by the passage of the Federal Trade Commission Act. The original intent of the act was to create an agency to enforce antitrust laws and protect businesses from each other. Originally, the FTC exercised little authority over advertising and marketing communications except in cases in which an advertisement would be considered unfair to the competition and would therefore restrict free trade.

In 1938, Congress passed the Wheeler-Lea Amendment to increase and expand the authority of the FTC. At that point, the agency was charged with the responsibility of stopping unfair or deceptive advertising practices and was allowed to levy fines when necessary. The law also granted the FTC access to the courts to enforce the law and follow up to be certain violators abide by FTC rulings.

An FTC investigation can be triggered through various types of complaints. These include problems noticed by

- consumers,
- businesses,
- Congress, and
- the media.

If any one of these raises a question about an unfair or deceptive practice, the FTC can intervene. Most investigations by the FTC are confidential at first. This protects both the agency and the company being investigated.

During the investigation, the FTC looks for unfair, deceptive, or false advertising. Any claims made by an advertiser must be carefully substantiated. An advertisement must have provable claims featuring valid evidence. If the advertisement is not substantiated or the FTC concludes that the ad is misleading, false, or deceptive based on the view of a typical consumer, then the FTC issues a consent order. If the company agrees to the consent order, an executive's signature indicates that the company agrees to discontinue the deceptive, false, or misleading advertisement. It is not an admission of guilt. They simply agree with the FTC to stop the ad.

If the company does not agree with the FTC and wishes to appeal or if the company does not stop the advertisement, the next step is an administrative hearing. As in a formal court trial, both sides are permitted to provide both written and oral testimony. If the judge rules in favor of the company the matter is dismissed. If the judge rules in favor of the FTC, a cease and desist order is issued whereby the company is ordered to discontinue the advertisement immediately and refrain in the future from running the ad or any similar advertisements.

The FTC can also issue trade regulation rulings that apply to an entire trade and not simply to one company. A trade regulation ruling is designed to stop what the FTC considers a deceptive or misleading practice by all or multiple firms within an industry.

FLANKER BRAND

A flanker brand is a new brand created by a company in a good or service category in which it currently has a brand offering. Flanker brands are used to help a company offer a more complete line of products. This creates barriers to entry for competing firms. Sometimes a flanker brand is introduced when company leaders believe that offering the product under the current brand name may adversely affect the current brand. This type of strategy is often used by firms in high-end markets who wish to compete in low-end markets. It is also used in international expansion. Offering different brands for specific markets is a common flanker brand strategy. This helps a firm to expand in an international market using more than their current brands. One of the largest companies to use flanker brands is Procter & Gamble.

FLIGHTING SCHEDULE (ADVERTISING CAMPAIGN)

A flighting schedule approach of advertising is characterized by running ads only during specific times of the year. No advertising is used between these spurts. For example, a retailer may run ads during peak times of the year, such as Christmas, but nothing during slower times of the year, such as January.

There are two primary flighting strategies. One is to run ads only during high-demand or peak seasons. The second is to run ads only during slow seasons. The philosophy behind the former strategy is to promote the brand name during the period in which the consumer or business is most likely to make a purchase. The latter strategy attempts to drum up business when purchases are not normally made. Running ads during slow periods is often designed to help create more stable production schedules and inventory levels. It may be used by a service to encourage a more stable use of facilities and to avoid overcrowding situations. Thus, a resort that is heavily booked during the summer may advertise only during the fall and winter in an effort to create visits during the off seasons.

FOCUS GROUP

A focus group normally consists of eight to ten people who are representative of the target market of an advertisement or advertising campaign. These individuals are paid in cash or are given financial incentives such as gift certificates to encourage them to participate. A trained moderator leads the group in discussing a particular product, advertisements, advertising campaign, or consumer behavior. The advantage of using a focus group is that it allows advertisers to probe consumers on why they think or act as they do.

Focus groups can be used to evaluate advertisements that already exist as well as new products that are being considered. They can also be established to discover consumer attitudes toward a brand name or company. Other focus groups are utilized to find out which marketing methods are most likely to be successful for a given product or service.

FOOD AND DRUG ADMINISTRATION

The Food and Drug Administration (FDA) regulates and oversees the packaging and labeling of products. The FDA also monitors advertising on food packages and advertisements for drugs, yet their primary responsibilities are ensuring food quality and drug safety. The FDA plays a role in the packaging and labeling of products, since any warning must be printed on the label.

FREESTANDING INSERT

Freestanding inserts (FSI) are sheets of coupons distributed in newspapers, primarily on Sunday. Nearly 80 percent of all manufacturer coupons are distributed through FSI. Many company executives prefer using FSI and print media to distribute coupons. They recognize that consumers must make a conscious effort to clip or save the coupon, which means it is more likely to be redeemed. Also, coupons create brand awareness as the consumer sees the brand name on the coupon even if they do not actually use the coupon. FSI encourage consumers to purchase brands on the next trip to the store. Manufacturers believe that consumers are more likely to purchase a couponed brand and remember the name when they redeem a coupon. This moves the brand to the consumer's long-term memory. When consumers recall a brand and buy it as the need arises, they do so even when they do not have that brand's coupons.[16]

FREQUENCY

Frequency is the average number of times an individual, household, or business within a particular target market is exposed to a particular advertisement within a specified time period, which is usually four weeks. Frequency can also refer to how many times a person was exposed to an ad during an advertising campaign, whether or not the person actually viewed the ad. The higher the frequency, the more likely a person will pay attention to a particular advertisement. For example, if an advertiser runs two ads on the evening news, and three ads on a television show such as *Friends,* this higher frequency increases the likelihood of the ad being seen by the firm's target market than if only one ad was shown on the evening news.

GATEKEEPER

A gatekeeper is the member of the business buying center who controls the flow of information to other members of the buying center. Also, gatekeepers keep buying center members informed about potential alternatives and help create the decision rules that are used in making purchasing decisions. It is the duty of the gatekeeper to let members know when various purchasing alternatives have been rejected. In some situations, the gatekeeper is not a specific individual. Instead, a gatekeeping function takes place, whereby members regulate the flow of information into the group, mutually establish decision rules, and reject alternatives. Also, when a gatekeeping function is performed by the group, each takes on the responsibility of keeping other members informed.

GENERATION X

Market segmentation by cohort groups based on age is a common tactic. Generation X is one of the generational cohorts that have been identified. The Generation X cohort consists of people who were born between approximately 1966 and 1976.

Reaching the Generation X cohort requires carefully designed advertisements. The most effective medium is the Internet rather than television. Also, the common elements present in this cohort apparently include some distaste for the values of the baby boom generation, which consists of many of the parents of individuals in Generation X.

Advertisements must be perceived as honest by Generation X to be effective. Puffery is not typically an effective tactic. Fantasy approaches and those focused on action tend to be more successful. (*See* SEGMENTATION BY GENERATION *for additional information.*)[17]

GENERIC MESSAGE STRATEGY

A message strategy is the primary tactic used in the creation of an advertising message. Message strategies can be divided into four categories: cognitive, affective, conative, and brand. The cognitive message strategies can, in turn, be divided into five subcategories: generic, preemptive, unique selling proposition, hyperbole, and comparative.

A generic message strategy is a direct promotion of a product's attributes or benefits without any claim of superiority. The goal of a generic message is to make the brand synonymous with the product category. This strategy works for brand leaders that are dominant within a given industry. Thus, Campbell's can declare "soup is good food" without any claim to superiority because they so strongly dominate the industry.

Generic message strategies are seldom found in business-to-business marketing messages, because few firms dominate industries. One major exception is Intel, which controls approximately 90 percent of the microprocessor market. The generic message "Intel inside" has been used for years to convey to businesses as well as end users the idea that the processor inside a computer was made by Intel and is therefore the best that is available. All computer manufacturers that utilize Intel processors are required to display the Intel logo, which illustrates the power a generic message has when a firm dominates the market.[18]

GEODEMOGRAPHIC SEGMENTATION

There are many ways to examine market segments for the purposes of creating advertising messages. Geodemographic segmentation combines census data (geographic data) with psychographic information. This is a powerful method for targeting a firm's customers because of its combination of census demographic information, geographic information, and psychographic information.

Geodemographic segmentation is often used by national firms conducting direct mail campaigns or sampling promotions. Through geodemographics, samples can be sent to the households that closely match the profile of a target market. For instance, colleges and universities use geodemographics to locate zip codes of communities that match student profiles.

PRIZM (Potential Rating Index by Zip Market) is a database that specializes in geodemographics. PRIZM consists of sixty-two different market segments in the United States. Every zip code within the United States has been categorized into the PRIZM database. PRIZM uses zip codes representing neighborhoods containing people with similar characteristics. Residents in various neighborhoods often share buying patterns. Recognizing that more than one market segment may live within a zip code, PRIZM identifies the largest market segments within each zip code.

GEOGRAPHIC SEGMENTATION

Geographic segmentation involves targeting a product to a specific region, such as the local neighborhood, city, county, trade area, or region of United States. This approach is often used by retailers. The customer base for most retail stores is normally confined to a specific geographic region surrounding the store. Geographic segmentation is also used in the business-to-business sector when customers are concentrated in a geographic area. An example of this concentration is the Silicon Valley area of California. Computer supply vendors often treat this geographic area as a distinct market segment.

GLOBALLY INTEGRATED MARKETING COMMUNICATIONS

Globally integrated marketing communications (GIMC) is integrated marketing communications (IMC) applied to an international company or global brand. The goal of GIMC is the same as IMC—to coordinate marketing efforts. The challenges, however, are greater due to larger national and cultural differences in target markets. In terms of an advertising strategy, perhaps the best philosophy to follow is "think globally but act locally." Advertising messages for global brands are often designed with a global theme, so the same general message is heard throughout the world. At the same time, advertisers routinely tailor or alter messages to fit the local culture and the target market. Two approaches to GIMC are standardization and adaptation. Standardization is using a common or global theme across nations. Adaptation is adjusting the message to a local area or target market.

GREEN MARKETING

Green marketing is the development and promotion of products that are environmentally safe. Most consumers favor the idea of green marketing. Surveys suggest that there is some consumer support for companies selling biodegradable products such as laundry detergents and trash bags. Numerous consumers also endorse recycling.

Green marketing programs generate positive publicity and word-of-mouth for a company. At the same time, only 10 percent of the population strongly supports environmentally safe products in the United States in terms of purchasing behaviors. Few consumers actually make purchase decisions based on criteria of environmental safety.[19] A reason for this was that for many years green marketing was associated with poor product quality and higher prices. For instance, originally, recycled paper was expensive, looked gray, and was inferior to regular paper. Early versions of environmentally safe fabric softeners clogged washing machines. Consequently, to succeed, green marketing will require firms to produce high-quality environmentally safe products at prices that are comparable to those of nongreen counterparts.

GROSS IMPRESSIONS

Gross impressions are the total number of exposures of an audience to an advertisement. They do not take into consideration what percentage of the total audience may or may not actually see the advertisement. Gross impressions are calculated by multiplying the number of ad insertions by the total readership of the magazine or, in the case of a television show, the number of people who watched a particular show during which the ad appeared. For example, assume the total readership of a magazine is approximately 21,051,000. If six ads were placed in that magazine, the gross impressions would be approximately 126 million.

GROSS RATING POINTS

Gross rating points (GRP) is a measure of the impact or intensity of a media plan. GRP is calculated by multiplying a vehicle's rating by the frequency or number of insertions of an advertisement. GRP provides the advertiser with a rough guideline about the chances that a chosen target audience actually sees an ad. Increasing the frequency of an advertisement or increasing the number of vehicles in which the ad is placed improves the odds that a consumer will see the advertisement. An advertisement that appears in each issue of a magazine such as *People* over a four-week period would be more likely to be seen than an advertisement that appears only once during that four-week period.

To calculate GRP, assume television show A had a rating of 8.3 and television show B had a rating of 4.8. If an advertiser had three ads on each show, the GRP for show A would be 24.9 (8.3 × 3), for show B it would be 14.4 (4.8 × 3), and a total GRP for the two programs and six ads would be 39.3 (24.9 + 14.4). (*See* RATINGS *for additional information.*)

HEDONIC EXPERIENTIAL MODEL

Hedonism is the tendency people have to maximize pleasure while minimizing pain. Following hedonic impulses often means ignoring longer-term consequences of behaviors while "giving in" to short-term pleasure. The hedonic experiential model (HEM) is an information processing model based on the concept that some purchasing decisions are made on the spur of the moment and are irrational. Such purchases are made because someone wants to have fun or to pursue a particular feeling, emotion, or fantasy. HEM effectively portrays emotions, or the affective component of attitude, which are the driving force for some purchases, rather than the mental or cognitive components of attitudes.

Information processing using HEM uses the same two routes (central and peripheral) that are used in the elaboration likelihood model (ELM). The primary difference, however, is found in the appeal or content of the message argument. ELM explains situations in which the consumer pays attention to the elements of the message argument pertaining to prices, company attributes, and product qualities or functions. The HEM approach portrays instances in which the consumer pays attention to elements of the message related to emotions, feelings, fun, and new or unusual experiences. Price advantages and making wise purchases are less important in those circumstances. (*See* ELABORATION LIKELIHOOD MODEL *for additional information.*)

HEREDITY AND HOME ENVIRONMENT

Heredity and the home environment are just two of the numerous factors that influence an individual's buying behaviors. Children are influenced by both heredity and their home environment and often make purchases in ways that are similar to those of their parents and other family members. The attitudes and values that are present in a home become strongly held, potentially lifelong features of the child's personality.

Heredity and home environment buying patterns can be illustrated using the baby boomer generation (persons born between 1945 and 1964). A common purchasing pattern exhibited by many baby boomers is substituting money and gifts for emotional support. This is due, in part, to the number of single-parent households in this generational cohort as well as the number of baby boomer households in which both spouses work. Intense time pressures take away time to spend with children. Instead, gifts and money are used to demonstrate love for a child. The children of baby boomers are now displaying the same type of behaviors as their parents. Such a learned behavior affects many homes. Consequently, advertisers can target goods, services, and messages to those affected by the guilt of not spending enough time with their kids, as well as other inherited and home environment issues.

HIERARCHY OF EFFECTS MODEL

One important activity in advertising is seeking to understand consumer behavior. The hierarchy of effects model is an aid in understanding consumer behavior. The model suggests that a consumer moves through a series of six steps in the process of making a purchase decision, which are

1. awareness,
2. knowledge,
3. liking,
4. preference,
5. conviction, and
6. the actual purchase.

The steps are considered to be sequential. A consumer will spend time at each step before moving on. This means a consumer develops a liking for a product after acquiring sufficient knowledge of the product, and knowledge only occurs after the consumer becomes aware of the specific product or brand. After liking comes preference, the stage at which the consumer favors a particular brand. Preference, however, does not necessarily result in a purchase. Before the actual purchase is made, a consumer must be convinced that a particular brand is superior or is the best value to purchase. Advertisers use the hierarchy of effects model to develop messages to aid in each step of the process.

In practical terms, advertising specialists recognize that in some instances consumers may first make a purchase and then later develop knowledge, liking, preference, and conviction. These are known as impulse buys or impulse purchases. It is also clear that shoppers sometimes purchase brands when no or little preference is involved, because coupons and other incentives cause them to buy. At other times, someone may not even remember what brand was purchased. However, the majority of purchases can be understood using the model. The hierarchy of effects model can also be used to describe the business-to-business purchase process. In business buying situations, the stages are followed by members of the buying center.

HUMOR APPEAL

A successful advertisement is one that reaches target consumers and causes them to remember the message. Humor is an effective technique for accomplishing these objectives because it has the ability to overcome advertising clutter. Humor is likely to capture a viewer's attention and consumers, in general, enjoy advertisements that make them laugh. Something that is funny also has intrusive value, which means it is able to grab attention. Humor is used in about 30 percent of all advertisements.[20]

As an advertising tactic, humor has three advantages. Humor causes consumers to (1) watch, (2) laugh, and (3) remember. Humorous ads are often easy to remember, which has been demonstrated in numerous recall tests. Once a humorous ad has attracted viewer interest, the same ad can lead to more careful consideration of the message. This occurs when the message is designed to increase comprehension and recall. Research indicates that humor elevates people's moods. An advertisement that creates a good mood can link the mood with the advertiser's products. Humor helps fix the company in the consumer's cognitive structure with links to positive feelings.[21]

To be successful, the humor should be directly connected to the product's benefits and it should tie together the product features, the advantage to customers, and the personal values of the means-ends chain. At the same time, advertisers are careful to avoid a situation in which the humor overpowers the message. When humor fails, it is usually because the joke in the ad is remembered but the product or brand is not. Although funny ads often win awards, they can fail in terms of accomplishing advertising objectives. To avoid this problem, the humor should relate to a product attribute, a customer benefit, or the personal value obtained from the product. The most effective uses of humor incorporate all three elements.

HYPERBOLE MESSAGE STRATEGY

A message strategy is the primary tactic used in the creation of an advertising message. Message strategies can be divided into four categories: cognitive, affective, conative, and brand. The cognitive message strategies, in turn, can be divided into five subcategories: generic, preemptive, unique selling proposition, hyperbole, and comparative.

In the development of an advertisement, the hyperbole message strategy approach makes an untestable claim based upon some product attribute or benefit. Most hyperbole statements rely on puffery. Such statements as "best," "greatest," and "finest" are examples of puffery. The Federal Trade Commission allows companies to make puffery statements as long as the message does not imply a specific product benefit or attribute. Consequently, advertisers will make sure puffery statements or hyperbole message strategies do not require substantiation or proof. (*See* FEDERAL TRADE COMMISSION *and* PUFFERY *for additional information.*)

IDENTIFICATION

When choosing a source or spokesperson, advertisers look for the ability to create identification. Identification occurs when the consumer is able to identify with the source, through fantasy, similar beliefs, common attitudes, preferences, or behaviors. Identification also occurs when the subject of a slice-of-life execution is placed in a situation that is the same or similar to the consumer's experience. For example, the frustration of having a stuffy nose is something most people can identify with. A medication that relieves the stuffy nose can then be more effectively marketed if the viewer can identify with the person in the ad. (*See* EXECUTIONAL FRAMEWORK; SOURCE CHARACTERISTICS; *and* SPOKESPERSONS AND SOURCES *for additional information.*)

IMAGE

Overall consumer perceptions or end user feelings toward the brand, company, or product being sold is the image. An image is formed based on every aspect of a company or brand. Advertising, product labels, and where the product is sold, as well as consumer interactions with employees all impact the brand or company image. Company leaders spend a considerable amount of time developing a positive, beneficial image for their organizations. Image is a vital part of long-term success. Advertising, public relations, and other marketing messages are integral components of a brand or corporate image. Through advertising, consumers can be influenced and the image of a brand or company shaped.

IMPRESSION MANAGEMENT

When executives discover that a negative story is circulating about a company, the goal is to respond in a manner that lessens the negative impact. Leaders of companies who have encountered negative press tend to behave in the same ways as any person would to protect a personal image. The tendency to protect one's self-image is called impression management. Impression management is the conscious or unconscious attempt to control images that are projected in real or imagined social interactions.

To maintain or enhance self-image, individuals and leaders of various organizations attempt to influence the identities they display to others. The goal is to project an image in a way that maximizes positive characteristics while minimizing any negative elements. Any event that threatens an image or desired identity is viewed as a predicament. When faced with a predicament, individuals make concerted efforts to reduce or minimize the negative consequences. If the predicament cannot be avoided or concealed, then an individual or company will engage in any type of remedial activity that reduces the potentially harmful consequences. Remedial tactics used by company leaders include[22]

- expressions of innocence,
- excuses, and
- justification.

An expression of innocence means management makes the claim that the negative event was not the company's fault. In fact, the company was an innocent party in the incident that occurred. The public should not blame the company for what happened. When management provides an excuse, the spokesperson provides reasons why the incident occurred, trying to vindicate the company and demonstrate that there were mitigating circumstances. A justification occurs when a representative of the company offers reasons for the company's actions. Although not admitting guilt, the company accepts responsibility for the incident but justifies why it occurred and how the company acted. The negative outcome was just an accident.

Impression management also includes emphasizing a positive image. Green marketing, social responsibility claims, altruistic activities, and other image-enhancing activities are publicized to give the impression that the company cares about its customers and the surrounding community.

IMPRESSIONS

See GROSS IMPRESSIONS.

IMPULSE DECISION

Consumers will often make an immediate decision to purchase a product with little or no forethought. Impulse purchases normally occur while the consumer is shopping in a retail store but can also occur when shopping on the Internet or viewing a direct marketing advertisement on television. In the retail environment, individuals may see a special display and make an immediate decision to buy something. In many stores, candy bars, gum, and magazines are usually placed near checkout registers because these items tend to be impulse buys.

Impulse purchases can occur for more expensive items. Clothes are sometimes purchased in this manner. Research indicates that when people travel on vacation, money has a different value. This leads to impulse buys of T-shirts, memorabilia, and other gift shop-type items, as well as food expenditures and other purchases that people would not ordinarily make.

Christmas is another time when people make impulsive decisions. Retailers routinely take advantage of impulse purchases. Items that may cause impulse buys are usually displayed at the front of the store, on center aisles, and in other highly visible places.

INFLUENCER

Influencers are members of the business buying center who shape purchasing decisions by providing the information or criteria utilized in evaluating alternatives. Often an influencer is formally appointed. The individual is selected by a committee charged with choosing a vendor. In other firms the process is less formal. For example, an engineer may describe the specifications for a particular product that his or her department needs and thus influence the decision.

Advertising messages often target influencers in business-to-business situations. Personal visits by sales representatives as well as other tactics are used to make sure the influencer carefully considers the vendor. Advertising can be used to reinforce the message sent to the influencer by the sales force. (*See* BUSINESS BUYING CENTER *for additional information.*)

INFORMATION SEARCH

The information search is the second step in the consumer decision making process. Once a need or want has been recognized, which is the first step, the consumer searches for information. An information search normally begins internally. The consumer mentally recalls images of products that might fulfill or meet a need. When the individual remembers how the need was satisfied in the past, he or she will be likely to recall the brand that was used. If that is associated with a positive experience, the consumer may simply repeat the purchase decision. This means the search stops at the internal level without further evaluation of alternatives. If the previous experience of a brand was negative, the consumer is likely to begin a more in-depth search. Exposures to other brands from past experiences and memories are then considered.

If an internal search does not provide enough information or a satisfactory solution, the consumer conducts an external search. Dissatisfaction with a previous purchase is not the only reason for an external search. The consumer may be exposed to a new brand or product or become enticed by the need for novelty or variety. Also, the consumer may consider a new brand because of a positive response to an advertisement.

From an advertising perspective, the search process is an important time to capture the consumer's attention. At that point, information about the company's brand should be presented in a convincing manner. The consumer's goal in making an external search is to acquire information leading to a better or more informed decision. Therefore, the goal of advertising is to provide information that helps the consumer believe buying the company's product is the best decision. The key is to provide convincing evidence or information at the right time. The message should include information about price, benefits, quality, image, or any other advantage that the company has over rival firms.

INFORMATIVE EXECUTION

Informative execution is a type of executional framework. Other types of executional frameworks include animation, slice-of-life, dramatization, testimonials, authoritative, demonstration, and fantasy. An informative execution presents information to the audience in a straightforward matter. Informative ads are used extensively on the radio, where only verbal communication is possible. They are less likely to be created for television or print, because consumers tend to ignore them. On television, it takes more than just the presentation of information to capture the consumer's attention. The same is true in print advertising.

High-involvement purchases are situations in which consumers will pay attention to an informational ad. This is true for both individnal consumers and businesses. Consumers buying stocks or mutual funds for retirement plans are more likely to be influenced by informative ads. When business buyers are in the process of gathering information for either a new buy or modified rebuy, a higher-involvement purchase is being made. When the business is not in the market for a particular product, buying center members do not pay as much attention to informative ads. Still, the informative framework continues to be a popular approach for business-to-business advertisers.

Effective informative executions rely on correct placement of the ad. An informative ad about a diet product in an issue of a magazine featuring a special article about weight control will be more readily noticed than a placement in the fashion section of the magazine. An informative business ad about lathes works well next to an article about the capital cost of equipment. Informative executions have limited uses but can be effective when placed properly. (*See* EXECUTIONAL FRAMEWORK *for additional information.*)

INGREDIENT BRANDING

Ingredient branding is a type of co-branding. Ingredient branding is the placement of one brand within another brand, such as Intel microprocessors in Compaq computers or NutraSweet in Pepsi drinks. The difficulty in ingredient branding is that the ingredient brand is usually lost in the process. Most automobiles owners have no idea what brand of battery, CD/stereo system, or tires were the original equipment on their automobiles, although these component parts kept their original brand names. To be effective, ingredient branding requires a strong brand name, such as Intel, so consumers believe the ingredient brand is important in the purchase decision. To achieve this prominence normally requires a heavy investment in advertising. (*See* CO-BRANDING *for additional information.*)

INTEGRATED MARKETING COMMUNICATIONS

Integrated marketing communications (IMC) is the coordination and integration of all marketing communication tools, avenues, and sources within a company into a seamless program that maximizes the impact on consumers and other end users at a minimal cost, which affects all of a firm's business-to-business, customer-focused, and internally oriented communications.[23]

Advertising is one component of IMC. It is important for a firm to speak with one voice and for a brand to have a unified message. Advertising must be developed in conjunction with the other components of the IMC. If the advertising function is being performed by an external advertising agency, it is critical that the advertising firm be apprised of the IMC plan and the role of advertising within that plan.

INTERNET ADVERTISING

Internet advertising is a recent phenomenon. It began with banner ads across computer screens as people visited the Web. Many experts believe that traditional banner ads had little influence on people. Consequently, Web designers attempt to attract attention using more elaborate banners. The use of graphics, flashing images, and streaming videos may help to garner attention.

Later, interstitial, or popup, ads were created. These ads forced Web browsers to react. Unfortunately, popup ads are controversial and are viewed as offensive by many. At the same time, advertisers know that popup ads are better at attracting buyers than traditional banner ads. This success has led many Internet companies to develop superstitials that work after a person leaves a Web site or even shuts off the computer. The ad will appear the next time the person logs onto the Internet.

Another form of Internet advertising is e-mail advertisements. These ads can be designed to include graphics and videos. Some Web users also object to e-mail advertisements even though advertisers know they work. The term "spam" has developed a strongly negative connotation.

As part of a worldwide Internet survey, respondents were asked to cite the most offensive form of advertising. Only 24 percent stated that no form of Internet advertising was intrusive or a turnoff. The biggest turn off was popup ads, named by 40 percent of the respondents. Next most disliked were e-mail ads at 28 percent. Banner ads bothered only 8 percent of the sample.[24]

Creativity is possible in Internet advertising because banners can be composed using many different types of graphics. Animation and streaming video may be incorporated into banner ads. Short lead time is possible because an advertisement can be changed and posted on the Internet immediately, even when ads are placed on other sites. Segmentation is easy to accomplish with the Internet. The company can track who is clicking on an advertisement and viewing various pages. Web surfers are often not aware that tracking has taken place and are often amazed that products they like suddenly appear on the screen.[25]

Web surfers tend to be young, well-educated, and have relatively high incomes. About 42 percent of Internet users are women and men are the other 58 percent. The average age is 34.9 years old. More than 65 percent of Internet users have household incomes of $50,000 or more, compared with 35 percent of the U.S. population as whole. In terms of education, 75 percent of Internet users have attended college compared to 46 percent of the general U.S. population.

The use of the Internet for business-to-business marketing has increased substantially. Placing ads on business sites is a new method of targeting ads to interested buyers. When employees are searching for product information, Internet ads will often be clicked on to see what is offered. Business buyers seeking product information pay more attention to ads they encounter while searching. Internet ads allow individual companies to advertise their own services.

INTERSTITIAL ADVERTISING

An interstitial advertisement is an Internet ad that interrupts a person on the Internet without warning. These types of ads must be clicked off to remove them from the screen. Interstitial ads are controversial because Web users feel they are annoying, especially when they appear on a person's computer even after the individual has logged off.

Although currently untested at this time, interstitial advertising may be useful in business-to-business markets. Ads that are sent to members of the buying center may attract attention without being annoying. Since the ads must be clicked off, the chances of capturing some level of attention from the employee increase. Also, if the business buyer has been searching for information about a product and an advertisement for that product pops up on the screen, the individual will likely study the ad to see what is being offered.

INTRUSION VALUE

Intrusion value is the ability of a medium or advertisement to intrude upon viewers without their voluntary attention. Intrusion can be accomplished using familiar music, a well-known and well-liked spokesperson, a startling picture of something unusual, or by featuring some form of sexual content. On the radio, a moment of silence may attract someone's attention as will a unique sound such as a soft drink being poured into a glass.

INVOLVEMENT

Involvement refers to the extent a stimulus or task is relevant to a consumer's existing needs, wants, or values. The more important a product is to a consumer, the more likely he or she will engage in an external search and pay attention to advertisements of that product. The level of involvement is based on several factors and will vary not only from one person to another but from product category to product category.

The primary factor impacting the level of involvement is the relative cost of the item. The higher the cost relative to a person's income, the higher the level of involvement. Also, the more important the item is to consumers, the higher will be their involvement.

Involvement may be enduring or situational. Enduring involvement is a consumer's continuing level of interest in a purchase. Situational involvement is based on a particular temporary situation. For example, buying clothes may be a low-involvement purchase for many teenage males (low enduring involvement), but choosing a tuxedo for the high school prom may cause a greater level of involvement (higher situational involvement).

JOINT DEMAND

Joint demand exists when component products are influenced by similar demand forces of related products. For example, the demand for transmissions at an automobile factory is related to demand for other component parts such as batteries, tires, spark plugs, and shock absorbers. A labor strike or work stoppage that interrupts the production of automobiles affects all of the manufacturer's suppliers. Thus, transmissions, tires, batteries, and other products used in the manufacturing of the automobile would be either reduced or stopped. Also, if the supply of one component used in the manufacture of a product is delayed, reduced, or stopped, the impact is felt on the demand for every component used in that product.

LEVERAGE POINT

A leverage point is the feature in an advertisement that leads the viewer to relate a product's benefits to personal values such as happiness, wisdom, social acceptance, excitement, and pleasure. To construct a quality leverage point, the creative must be able to build a pathway that connects a product's benefit to the potential buyer's value system.

The leverage point in a print advertisement normally consists of a headline designed to catch the reader's attention. The headline is also tied into the copy of the advertisement. Leverage points in other media, such as television and radio, can be assisted by liking of the spokesperson, the music presented in the ad, and other elements such as the background in a television commercial.

Quality leverage points are important in both consumer and business-to-business advertisements. Business ads must appeal to the personal values of members of the buying center, which may include feelings of loyalty to the company making the purchase.

MAGAZINE ADVERTISING

Magazines have been a second choice for many advertisers because the glamour of television has overshadowed magazines. Recent research indicates that, in some cases, magazines are actually a better option. A study by the ACNielson Company revealed that people who viewed ads in magazines were from 2 to 37 percent more likely to purchase the product.

The primary advantage of magazine advertising is the ability to target various market segments. Magazines are often oriented to fairly specific topic areas. Specialized magazines with highly targeted audiences are more common than general magazines with broad readerships. For many market segments, such as automobiles, a number of magazines exist. Because magazines are so highly differentiated, high audience interest becomes another advantage. For example, an individual who subscribes to *Modern Bride* has some level of attraction to weddings.

Magazines offer high-quality color and sophisticated production processes. This provides the creative with the opportunity to produce intriguing and enticing advertisements. Motion, color, and unusual images can be used to attract attention. Some magazines will include scratch-and-sniff ads to entice readers to notice the fragrance of a perfume or cologne. Even car manufacturers have ventured into this type of advertising by producing a smell of leather in certain ads.

People reading magazines also tend to view and pay attention to advertisements that relate to their needs and wants. Often readers will linger over an ad longer, since magazines are sometimes read in a waiting situation (e.g., doctor's office) or during a person's leisure time. This high level of interest, segmentation, and differentiation is ideal for products with precisely defined target markets.

Both trade and business journals are a major medium for business-to-business marketing. A greater level of detail can be provided in the copy, and interested readers often take the time to read the information. Toll-free telephone numbers and Web addresses are also provided in print ads. Businesses are able to target their advertisements in key trade journals that are most likely to be read by members of the buying center.

Magazine advertisements have a long life. Magazines are often read and reread by subscribers, which means advertisements will often be seen more than once. This appeal is attractive to advertisers because they know the reader is exposed multiple times and will likely pay more attention to the ad.

MARKET SEGMENTATION

A market segment is a set of businesses or group of individual consumers with distinct characteristics. Market segmentation is the process of locating and dividing the market into specific groups based on their needs, attitudes, and interests. The advantages of market segmentation include helping marketers identify company strengths and weaknesses as well as opportunities in the marketplace. A market segment helps the company work toward the goal of matching what the firm does best with the most likely customers. Market segments are used to clarify marketing objectives associated with individual target markets. Also, the marketing team can more precisely focus budgeting expenditures on profitable consumer groups and business segments. Identifying important market segments makes it possible to link company strategies and tactics to subsequent marketing activities.

For a market segment to be considered a viable target for an advertising campaign, it should meet the following tests:

- The individuals or businesses within the market segment should be similar in nature, having similar needs, attitudes, interests, and opinions. This means persons or businesses within the segment are homogenous.
- The market segment differs from the population as a whole. Segments are distinct from other segments and the general population.
- The market segment must be large enough to be financially viable to target with a separate advertising campaign.
- The market segment must be reachable through some type of media or advertising communications method.

MARKETING MIX

The marketing mix consists of product, price, place (the distribution system), and promotion. Promotional activities include advertising, sales promotions, and personal selling. The sales promotion area normally includes both sales and trade promotions, where sales promotions are aimed at end users or consumers of goods and services and trade promotions are directed toward distributors and retailers. Within the context of promotions, some marketing experts would add direct marketing activities and public relations programs. Others would instead include them within the three major components of advertising, sales promotions, and personal selling.

MEANS-ENDS CONCEPTUALIZATION
OF COMPONENTS FOR ADVERTISING STRATEGY

Means-ends conceptualization of components for advertising strategy (MECCAS) is an advertising development approach which suggests that designing an advertisement includes the following five elements:[26]

1. The product's attributes
2. Consumer benefits
3. Leverage point
4. Personal values
5. The executional framework

The MECCAS approach suggests that in designing an advertisement, the goal is to move consumers through the first four elements sequentially from the product's attributes to personal values. The last element, the executional framework, is the manner or method in which this process is accomplished.

The first step is to identify the attributes of a product and link them to specific benefits consumers can acquire from using or purchasing the product. These benefits are then attached to a consumer's personal value system using some type of leverage point. The leverage point is the cue in the advertisement that connects the benefit to the value system in such a manner that the person moves from appreciating the product's attributes and/or benefits to his or her personal values. (*See* EXECUTIONAL FRAMEWORK *and* LEVERAGE POINT *for additional information.*)

MEANS-ENDS THEORY

Means-ends theory, or a means-ends chain, is derived from the idea that an advertisement message contains a means, which is a reasoning or mental process, that leads the consumer to a desired end state. End states consist of personal values for consumers and business values in the case of a business-to-business advertisement. These values are ends that an individual or company desires to reach. Personal values may include the following:

- Comfortable life
- Equality
- Excitement
- Freedom
- Fun
- Happiness
- Health
- Love
- Personal accomplishment
- Pleasure
- Salvation
- Security
- Self-fulfillment
- Self-respect
- Sense of belonging
- Social acceptance
- Wisdom

A means-ends chain is designed to cause a chain reaction. Viewing an advertisement should lead the consumer to believe that using the product will help the individual achieve one or more personal values.

For instance, an advertisement for a wrinkle cream may highlight the product's ability to make a person's skin smoother. The consumer may then be led to purchase the antiwrinkle cream based on the belief that it will lead to healthier skin. Healthy skin, in turn, may enhance personal feelings of self-respect and social acceptance. The motivation for the purchase is not the product attribute, but rather the benefit the product produces, in this case wrinkle-free skin and the resulting end, which is a higher level of self-respect and a higher level of social acceptance by others. Means-ends chains are often used in slice-of-life and dramatization executions. Reaching the value is the end point of a problem being resolved by the product.

MEDIA BUYER

The person who buys space, negotiates rates and times, and schedules advertisements is the media buyer. Media buyers are employed by advertising agencies, media firms, and individual companies. Media buyers work in conjunction with media sales representatives. Media buyers study advertising rates and schedules. They look for special deals and create tie-ins between primary and secondary media outlets, such as finding radio television stations that are owned by the same organization or person.

A media buyer works carefully with the media planner, creative, and account executive in the design of an advertising campaign to ensure that promotional dollars are spent wisely. Each individual plays a crucial role in the development of an advertising campaign and a company's integrated marketing communications (IMC) program. The challenge of coordinating the efforts of these individuals intensifies when they are from different companies.

MEDIA MIX

A media mix is the combination of advertising outlets that has been selected for an advertising campaign. Choosing the appropriate advertising channels and effectively combining those outlets requires the expertise of a media planner. The media planner studies the outlets individually and collectively and matches them with the product and overall message. Both media planners and media buyers are excellent sources of information regarding the type of mix that will be most effective for a particular advertising campaign. It then becomes the challenge for the creative to design ads for each medium. The ads should speak to the audience and tie in with the overall theme of the integrated advertising campaign. (*See* MEDIA BUYER *and* MEDIA PLANNER *for additional information.*)

MEDIA MULTIPLIER EFFECT

The media multiplier effect is a theory that suggests that the impact of two or more media is stronger than using either medium alone. An advertising campaign that runs in magazines and on television would be stronger than one that uses only television or only magazines. Seeing the same ad in different media increases the retention and recall rates of an advertisement.

The media multiplier effect is related to choices in creating a media mix. Many times a primary medium is chosen in conjunction with one or more supporting or secondary media. The goal is to make certain the consumer is exposed to the message in more than one venue.

MEDIA PLANNER

The primary job of the media planner is to outline a program stating where and when to place advertisements. Media planners work closely with creatives and account executives. The creative must know which media will be used because they have a major impact on how advertisements will be designed. Television ads, for example, are designed differently than radio or newspaper ads.

One of the primary tasks of the media planner is to conduct research to match the product's target market with the right media target market. A target market of thirty-five- to fifty-year-old females with college degrees will be reached with media that are far different from those used to attract eighteen- to twenty-five-year-old males who are not college educated. In addition to locating the right media,

media planners will try to find optimal locations within a medium for an advertisement. Consequently, a fishing magazine will contain advertisements for bass boats and fishing gear next to articles about the summer feeding habits of bass and other fish, because the successful media planner has identified these ideal locations for advertisements.

MEDIA PLANNING

Media planning is the process of plotting the choices of media that a specific, defined target market is likely to experience through the course of a typical day. Media planning begins with a careful analysis of the target market.

One common method of media planning is approaching it from the customer's viewpoint. Although demographics such as age, gender, income, and education are important, they are not enough to determine the media habits of people in a target market. Discovering the viewing patterns of these customers means messages can be designed to appeal to them more effectively. Also, key consumers can be reached at specific times and locations with carefully crafted advertising messages. Specific details about target market customers are extremely valuable in developing a media strategy.

Several individuals are involved in media planning. Account executives, creatives, media planners, and media buyers all provide input. In smaller advertising agencies, the media planner and media buyer may be the same person. In larger companies, they are normally different individuals.

MEDIA SERVICE COMPANY

Media service companies negotiate and purchase media packages, called media buys. These companies have expertise in making media buys and understand the profile of each medium. Advertising agencies often rely on media service agencies to handle this portion of the ad campaign for them. For companies who do their own advertising work, media service companies are normally used to ensure that the best media buys are made.

MEDIA STRATEGY

The media strategy is the process of analyzing and choosing media for an advertising campaign. The strategy must take into account several factors as it is being put together, including (1) the objectives of the campaign, (2) the target audience, (3) the message theme (the key message to be conveyed to target markets), and (4) other constraints and considerations, such as the overall integrated marketing communications objectives and legal restrictions. These guidelines are created so that the advertising creative, account executive, media buyer, media planner, and company representatives can decide which media are best for a campaign. They should also seek out logical combinations of media for advertising messages. Both primary and secondary media should be chosen as part of a media strategy.

MESSAGE EVALUATION

The purpose of a message evaluation is to determine if the advertisement will have the desired effect on the intended audience. Evaluation or testing of advertising communications occurs at any stage of development. The first place to test an advertisement is the concept stage. These tests are used before the ad is produced. The testing involves soliciting opinions from experts or from average consumers.

A second point at which an ad can be tested is after the design stage, which is prior to development. Television ads may be produced using storyboards, which consist of still photographs or sketches that outline the structure of the ad. The third time an ad can be tested is after the commercial has been produced. At that stage, experimental tests can be used to evaluate the ad. To do so, a group of consumers is invited to watch the ad in a theater-type setting. The test ad is placed in a grouping of ads to disguise it. Viewers are then asked to evaluate all of the ads, including the test ad, to see if the test ad had the desired effect. Before launching the campaign, an advertising agency may show the ad in a test market area. Several tools can then be used to measure the quality and impact of the ad.

The final stage of evaluation takes place after the marketing communication has been used. Information collected at this point helps the marketing team assess what worked and what did not. Several methods are available to those who investigate the message content of an advertisement:

- Concept testing
- Copytesting
- Recall tests
- Recognition tests
- Attitude and opinion tests
- Emotional reaction tests
- Physiological arousal tests
- Persuasion tests

Most of these methods deal with the verbal or written components of an advertisement. Also, peripheral cues are important and should be tested.

The best method to use in message evaluation depends on the objective of the advertising plan. Most advertisers use more than one method to make sure the findings are as accurate as possible. In testing ads that have run, it is also wise to use both a pre- and posttest to be able to compare before and after scores to more accurately measure the impact of the ad campaign.

MESSAGE STRATEGY

A message strategy is the primary tactic used in the development of an advertisement. The message strategy determines what message theme will be used. There are four broad categories of message strategies:[27]

1. Cognitive strategies
2. Affective strategies
3. Conative strategies
4. Brand strategies

Cognitive message strategies are based on rational arguments and rely on cognitive processing of an advertisement. Affective strategies are based on feelings or emotions and are designed to have an impact on the affective component of attitude. Conative message strategies are designed to encourage a viewer to act or behave in a particular manner. Brand message strategies place a high emphasis on the brand being advertised with the goal of building either brand recognition or brand affinity. *(See each of the message strategies for additional information.)*

MESSAGE THEME

A key component of a creative brief is the message theme, which is an outline of the key idea or ideas that the campaign or advertisement conveys. Often a message theme is the promise of a benefit. For example, a hotel chain may try to express the message theme of luxury.

Message themes can utilize both emotional and rational processes. A rational theme emphasizes logical benefits, such as cavity protection in a toothpaste. An emotional theme is more likely to be abstract and focus on images and feelings that are benefits associated with using a product. The message theme will be matched to the advertising medium chosen, the target market, and the nature of the company's product and brand. *(See* CREATIVE BRIEF *for additional information.)*

MODIFIED REBUY

A modified rebuy refers to a business-to-business buying situation in which company leaders or members of the buying center consider and evaluate alternatives before the purchase is made. Modified rebuys occur for four reasons. First, if company leaders are dissatisfied with a current vendor they may want to look at other options. The greater the level of dissatisfaction, the stronger will be the desire to examine new possibilities.

Second, if a new company offers what appears to be a better buy, the purchase decision may be reconsidered. The new option may be a superior quality product or one offered at a lower price. The terms of purchase being offered by a new company may be more attractive. Finally, when a new vendor is perceived as superior or more dependable than a current vendor, members of the buying center may take a look at the new company.

A third condition that creates a modified rebuy is the end of a contractual agreement. It is common for company policies to state that competing bids must be considered for each new contract period. This is true for most governmental organizations. The amount of time spent in the buying process depends on how satisfied a company is with a current vendor and the time it takes to compare the company's current vendor with other potential vendors.

The fourth modified rebuy situation occurs when a company purchases a good or service with which leaders have only limited or infrequent experience. This is especially likely when prices, product features, or vendors change over time. In most cases, the composition of the buying group also changes. In each case, the decision to reconsider depends on the desires of members of the buying center.

MOTIVATION (INFORMATION SEARCH)

In a purchase decision, the degree to which an external search for information takes place partly depends on a customer's level of motivation. The higher a consumer's motivation level, the more he or she will conduct an external search for additional evaluation information. The level of motivation is determined by

- the consumer's level of involvement,
- the customer's need for cognition, and
- the customer's level of shopping enthusiasm.

The higher the level of involvement in the purchase, the more motivated an individual will be to search for information. For example, buying a gift for someone important is likely to trigger a higher level of involvement and greater motivation to search for just the right gift, especially when the gift recipient is a loved one or a person the buyer wishes to impress. In these circumstances, the consumer will seek out additional information about purchasing alternatives.

Individuals who have a high level of cognition will be more motivated to search for information. Cognition in this sense refers to the person's desire to gather facts before making a decision. These individuals think things through and will make a decision only after mental effort. They seldom make any irrational or impulse decisions. Finally, people who enjoy shopping tend to search for more information than people who do not like shopping.

MULTIATTRIBUTE APPROACH

In evaluating purchase alternatives, one method consumers use is called the multiattribute approach. The key to understanding this model is noting that consumers often examine sets of attributes across sets of products or brands. The multiattribute model assumes that a consumer's attitude toward a brand is determined by the consumer's beliefs about a brand's performance on various attributes that are important in the purchase decision. It is also assumed in the model that attributes vary in importance to the consumer. Thus, the higher a brand is rated on attributes that are important to the consumer, the more likely it becomes that the brand will be purchased.

In using the multiattribute approach, a consumer first determines what attributes are important. For instance, in the purchase of an automobile, a consumer may decide gas mileage, price, styling, and color are important criteria. In most cases, the criteria have different weights. In other words, gas mileage may be the most important and styling second. Color and price may tie for third, or color may be slightly higher than price.

The buyer then rates each automobile along these four criteria. The model that is chosen is usually the one with the best overall score. It is unlikely that one brand will get the top score in every category. For example, car A may have the best gas mileage but may be second or third in terms of styling. The car that has the best styling may be second in gas mileage and rank high in color and price. It may actually be chosen because the consumer sees it as the overall best choice. The multiattribute approach recognizes that there are trade-offs between the brands being evaluated and the criteria used for selection. (*See* AFFECT REFERRAL *and* EVOKED SET *for additional methods of evaluating purchase alternatives.*)

MUSICAL APPEAL

Music is an extremely important component of many advertisements. In some advertisements music is a peripheral cue, whereas in others it is the primary theme. A musical appeal uses music as a key component in the design of an advertisement. Music gains attention and increases the retention of visual information at the same time.

Music helps capture the attention of listeners and is linked to emotions, memories, and other experiences, especially if a familiar song is used. Music can be intrusive, thereby gaining the attention of someone who was previously not listening to or watching a program. Music can be the stimulus that ties a particular musical arrangement, jingle, or song to a particular product or company. As soon as the tune begins, consumers know what product is being advertised because they have been conditioned to tie the product to the music. Music can also increase the persuasiveness of argument. When subjects were asked to compare ads with music to identical ads without music, those with music almost always rated higher in terms of persuasiveness.[28]

Several decisions are made when selecting music for ads. They include answering questions such as these:

- What role will music play in the ad?
- Will a familiar song be used, or will something original be created?
- What emotional pitch should the music reach?
- How does the music fit with the message of the ad?

The creative must select the correct type of music, from whimsical to dramatic to romantic, to match the content of the advertisement. A quality match between the music and the ad theme can lead to a strong favorable reaction by the viewer or listener. Also, just as the wrong plot or wrong actors in an advertisement can mean disaster, selecting the wrong music can have a negative impact.

Another important decision involves the selection of a familiar tune versus creating original music for the ad. The most common method is to write a jingle or music specifically for the advertisement.

Background or mood-inducing music is usually instrumental, and advertisers often pay musicians to write music that matches the scenes in the ad.

Using a well-known song has advantages. The primary benefit is that consumers already have an affinity for the song. This emotional attachment may be transferred to the product. Brand awareness, brand equity, and brand loyalty are easier to develop when consumers are familiar with the music. Many times, an existing song is adapted for an ad.[29]

NATIONAL ADVERTISING DIVISION

The National Advertising Division (NAD) is a subunit of the Better Business Bureau. Complaints about advertising are referred to the NAD for review. The role of the NAD is to determine if an advertisement is false, misleading, or in some other way unethical. Members of the NAD will collect and evaluate information concerning any complaint about a company's advertisements. A primary responsibility of the NAD is to determine if an advertising claim can be substantiated. If it is not, the NAD negotiates with the business to modify or discontinue the advertisement. If the firm's advertising claim is substantiated, then the complaint is dismissed. Both individuals and companies can file complaints about unfair ads with the NAD. (*See* BETTER BUSINESS BUREAU *for additional information.*)

NATIONAL ADVERTISING REVIEW BOARD

The National Advertising Review Board (NARB) is a subunit of the Better Business Bureau. The NARB is composed of advertising professionals and prominent civic-minded individuals. The NARB plays a role when a complaint about an advertisement has not been resolved by the National Advertising Division (NAD) of the Better Business Bureau. The NARB also becomes involved if an advertiser appeals the decision of the NAD.

In the case of an advertisement dispute, if the NARB rules that the firm's advertisements are not substantiated, an order is issued demanding that the firm discontinue the advertisements. Such an order is similar to a consent order filed by the Federal Trade Commission (FTC). The primary difference is that the NARB is a private board rather than a government agency. Therefore, if a firm being accused of a false or misleading advertisement refuses to accept an NARB ruling the matter is turned over to the FTC or some other federal regulatory agency. It is important to note that the NARB does not always rule in favor of the firm or consumer making a complaint about an advertisement. Occasionally the NARB will reverse a ruling by the NAD. The NARB rarely refers a case to the FTC. In the final twenty-five years of the twentieth century, only four such actions were taken. (*See* BETTER BUSINESS BUREAU *and* NATIONAL ADVERTISING DIVISION *for additional information.*)

NEWSPAPER ADVERTISING

A traditional advertising outlet for many companies is the newspaper. Newspapers vary from small, local market weekly editions to major city daily editions to tabloids. More recently, many newspapers may be found online. Also, *The Wall Street Journal* and *USA Today* are essentially national daily newspapers. The newspaper business has become extremely competitive. Many small local papers no longer exist and most major city newspaper chains are owned by conglomerates such as Gannett. Newspapers remain an important advertising venue.

Many types of retailers rely on newspapers ads. Newspapers offer geographic selectivity as well as access to local markets in many communities. Promoting sales, retail hours, and store locations is easy in a newspaper ad. Short lead time allows retailers to change ads and promotions quickly. This flexibility is a strong advantage. It allows advertisers to keep ads current. Also, advertisements can be modified to meet competitive offers or to focus on recent events.

Newspapers have high levels of credibility. Readers rely on newspapers for factual information and hold high interest levels in newspaper stories. Twenty-four-hour television news stations and Internet sites such as CNN have changed the nature of newspaper reporting.

Many in-depth stories are written with accompanying graphs and sidebars to fully review an issue, rather than providing basic details. This means subscribers tend to pay more attention to advertisements as well as the news stories. This increased audience interest allows advertisers to provide more copy detail in advertisements. Newspaper readers take more time to read copy, unless too much information is jammed into a small space.

Newspaper advertisers receive volume discounts for buying more column inches of advertising space. Many newspapers grant these volume discounts, called cumulative discounts, over one-month, three-month, or even year-long periods. This potentially makes the cost per exposure even lower, since larger and repeated ads are more likely to garner the reader's attention.

Many local consumers rely heavily on newspaper advertising for information about grocery specials and other similar price discounts. Newspaper coupons are also offered by local merchants. Special response features ("Mention our ad in today's paper, and receive 10 percent off") are also popular with local advertisers.

Business-to-business advertisements appear in metropolitan newspapers as well as national daily papers. They offer the opportunity to provide more lengthy descriptions of goods and services being sold to other companies.

NEW-TASK PURCHASE

In business-to-business buying situations, a new-task purchase occurs when a company is buying a good or service for the first time and the product involved is one with which the company's buyers have no experience. This type of purchase normally requires input from a number of people in the buying center. Considerable time is spent gathering information and evaluating vendors. In many cases, vendors are asked to assist in identifying the specifications that will be required. The circumstances are different than a straight rebuy, in which a previous purchase has been made, or a modified rebuy, in which only a limited search will be undertaken. New-task purchases require the most effort and cause more expenses for the purchasing firm. Therefore, they are normally limited to more major expenditures. (*See also* BUSINESS BUYING CENTER; MODIFIED REBUY; *and* STRAIGHT REBUY *for additional information.*)

NOISE

Noise is anything that distorts or disrupts a message being sent from a sender to a receiver. It can occur at any stage in the communication process, including the encoding, transmission, or decoding stages. Noise takes a variety of forms, from loud rooms where it is difficult to hear to fundamental differences between a sender and a receiver, such as a highly educated individual using technical terminology with someone with a lower level of cognition.

Noise is part of the advertising world. An example of noise is the large number of ads in a magazine, which distracts the reader from focusing on a single ad. Also, someone talking during a television ad means the ad is less likely to be noticed and remembered. Rush hour traffic on highways causes a type of noise that makes it less likely that a driver will notice a billboard.

Advertisers will spend a considerable amount of time and thought in designing an advertisement that overcomes the noise associated with clutter. Also, a clear and powerful message helps the advertiser overcome other forms of noise. (*See also* CLUTTER *and* COMMUNICATION *for additional information.*)

OPINION TEST

See ATTITUDE OR OPINION TEST.

OPPORTUNITY ANALYSIS

An opportunity analysis is a component of a communications market analysis. The goal of an opportunity analysis is to discover new marketing and/or communication opportunities. Typical questions that are helpful in conducting an opportunity analysis include these:

1. Are there customers that the competition is ignoring or not serving?
2. Which markets are heavily saturated and have intense competition?
3. Are the benefits of our goods and services being clearly articulated to our customers?
4. Are there opportunities to build relationships with customers using a slightly different marketing approach?
5. Are there opportunities that are not being pursued, or is our brand positioned with a cluster of other companies in such a manner that it cannot stand out?

The final result of an opportunity analysis should be to reveal communication opportunities that can be exploited. They should identify unfilled market niches, places when the competition is doing a poor job of meeting the needs of some customers, and situations in which the company has a distinct competence or some other advantage to offer.

OUTDOOR ADVERTISING

The many forms of outdoor advertising include signs on cabs, buses, park benches, and any surface within or surrounding a sports arena. A blimp flying over a major sporting event is also a form of outdoor advertising. The most common form of outdoor advertising, however, is billboards. Billboards are placed along major roads, on buildings, and in other locations near flows of traffic.

One primary advantage of outdoor and billboard advertising is its long life. Space on a billboard is normally rented for one month or more. The result is that in terms of cost per impression, outdoor advertising is relatively inexpensive. Outdoor advertising also offers a broad reach and a high level of frequency when multiple billboards are purchased. Every person who passes by a billboard has the potential of being exposed to the message. Many billboard companies provide rotation packages, in which an ad moves to different locations throughout a city, county, or state during the course of the year, thereby increasing the reach of the ad.

For local companies, billboards are an excellent advertising medium. Messages can be prepared for and tailored to local audiences. Restaurants, hotels, resorts, service stations, and amusement parks often heavily utilize billboards. Billboards provide an effective way to communicate a firm's location to travelers. Individuals who want to eat at a particular restaurant (such as Wendy's, Shoney's, or Burger King) while on the road can normally spot a billboard for that restaurant.

The typical design of a billboard ad is large and spectacular. The large size of most billboards helps make them major attention-getting devices. Also, the large size creates the impression that the product and message are important. Movement and lighting add to the attention-capturing qualities of billboards.

Billboards are used as both primary and secondary media in advertising campaigns. Their usage depends on the size and location of the company as well as the goal of the message. Longer, more complicated messages normally do not appear in outdoor advertisements.

PERSUASION

One of the most common goals of advertising campaigns is persuasion, and the primary goal of persuasive advertisements is to convince consumers that a particular brand is superior. Persuasive ads may also be used to show consumers the negative consequences of failing to use a particular brand.

Causing a change in consumer attitudes and persuading people to consider a new purchasing choice is challenging. The typical tactic begins with unfreezing previous attitudes, which makes the consumer open to the possibility of change. Next, an alternative is offered. Finally, the goal is to "refreeze" or instill the new attitude about the product in the consumer's mind.

Persuasive advertising is used more in consumer marketing than in business-to-business situations. More rational appeals are used in business advertisements. Also, persuasion techniques are more frequently prepared for broadcast media such as television and radio than for outdoor or print advertising.

PERSUASION ANALYSIS EVALUATION

When a persuasive advertisement is prepared, it is important to make certain the ad is having the desired effect. Persuasion evaluation techniques require a pre- and posttest assessment procedure. This process begins by measuring people's attitudes prior to being exposed to an advertisement and then after the exposure to detect any attitudinal changes.

One technique to assess the persuasiveness of a television advertisement starts by gathering a group of consumers in a theater. Measures of brand attitudes and purchase intentions are then taken for the test brand and other brands that are part of the study. A series of commercials is then shown as part of a program. Next, measures are used to identify any changes in attitudes or purchase intentions. The amount of change indicates whether or not the persuasion in the advertisement worked.

The ultimate goal of persuasion is a change in purchase intentions and actual purchase behaviors. Therefore, it is important to assess actual behaviors to confirm the predictive value of persuasion tests whenever possible.

PHYSIOLOGICAL AROUSAL TEST

Many times, advertisers are interested in eliciting emotional responses in their messages. Physiological arousal tests measure the fluctuations in a person's body functions that are associated with changing emotions. The most common types of physiological arousal tests are conducted using a psychogalvanometer, a pupillometric test, or a voice-pitch analysis.

A psychogalvanometer measures a person's perspiration levels in the palm and fingers. A person being affected by an advertisement often responds with a change in levels of sweat. This arousal indicates interest and an emotional reaction. An emotional reaction can be negative or positive. The galvanometer measures the individual's perspiration level.

A pupillometric meter is designed to measure pupil dilation. Dilation levels change with emotional arousal. When pupils dilate, the subject is experiencing a positive reaction to the advertisement. The subject's pupils will become smaller when the reaction is negative.

The voice-pitch method examines changes in the pitch of a person's voice as the individual reacts with emotion. The actual voice-pitch device utilizes special computer software. The assumption is that a more shrill or higher-pitched voice suggests a stronger response. The technique involves measuring a person's voice pitch as the individual answers a series of questions. When the person's vocal cords tighten, the pitch of his or her voice is higher, suggesting the person has been emotionally affected. The amount of change in the pitch indicates how strongly the person has been influenced.

These three tests are based on the assumption that emotions affect people physiologically and that these physical responses can be measured. Some researchers believe physiological arousal tests are more accurate than emotional reaction tests, because physiological arousal cannot easily be faked.

To demonstrate the potential advantage of physiological tests, consider an advertisement with a sexually attractive model. In a focus group, some participants may enjoy the ad but hide their true reactions, stating the ad is sexist and inappropriate. Social pressure or the desire for acceptance in the group may drive such a reaction. These same individuals may not move the joystick to report true reactions when participating in a study using the warmth monitor because of the potential stigma attached to sex in advertising that often affects self-reported reactions. A physiological arousal test allows the subject to behave in a socially acceptable manner while the measures may more accurately indicate the person's actual response.

POINT-OF-PURCHASE ADVERTISING

Point-of-purchase (POP) advertising is any form of special display in a retail store that features or advertises merchandise. These displays are located near cash registers, at the ends of aisles, in a store's entryway, or in other noticeable places. The many forms of POP advertising include displays, signs, structures, and devices that identify, advertise, and/or merchandise an outlet, service, or product. POP programs are used to stimulate retail sales or activity. The store shelf and POP display represent the last chance for the manufacturer to reach the consumer. They can be used to make an impression just before a purchase is made, or to leave an impression when the buyer exits the store.

POP displays are highly effective tools because nearly 50 percent of the money spent by consumers at mass merchandiser and supermarket locations is unplanned. Research indicates that an average increase in sales of 10 percent occurs when one POP display is used and 22 percent when there are two. Consequently, POP advertising is very attractive to manufacturers.[30] The largest users of POP advertising are restaurants, food services, apparel stores, and footwear retailers. The fastest growing categories are fresh, frozen, or refrigerated foods and professional services.[31] Whereas manufacturers view POP displays as an attractive method of getting their brand more prominently displayed before customers, retailers have a different perspective. Retailers are most inclined to set up only the POP displays that best suit store sales objectives.

To be effective, POP displays must communicate the product's attributes clearly. The best POP displays are those that are integrated with the other marketing messages. Logos and message themes used in advertisements normally appear on the POP along with any form of special sales promotion. Many times a POP display only has three-tenths of second to capture the customer's attention. If it fails, the customer simply moves on to other merchandise. Colors, designs, merchandise arrangements, and tie-ins with other marketing messages are critical elements of effective POP displays.

PORTFOLIO TEST

A portfolio test is a method for evaluating messages presented in an advertisement. In a portfolio test, subjects are normally shown a set of print ads or view a set of television ads (the portfolio) and are asked to evaluate the ads in that portfolio. Individuals who participate in the test do not know which advertisement is under scrutiny.

A portfolio test is designed to mimic reality in a manner similar to the ways consumers are normally exposed to multiple messages as in a magazine or newspaper. The reader encounters numerous ads throughout the magazine or newspaper. The portfolio test helps researchers to compare a target piece of advertising with other ads. For the portfolio test to yield the optimal findings, it is essential that all of the advertisements shown are in the same stage of development. For example, if the test ad is still in the draft stage, then the other ads used in the portfolio should also be in the draft stage.

POSITIONING ADVERTISING COPYTESTING

Positioning advertising copytesting (PACT) is an evaluation method that was developed to assess various television advertisements. PACT was formulated by twenty-one leading U.S. advertising agencies.[32] Although PACT normally examines the issues involved in copytesting television ads, the principles can be used for any type of advertising message. The PACT principles are an excellent guideline to evaluating an advertising message and are also worthwhile to keep in mind as an advertising message is being designed. PACT has nine principles:

1. The testing procedure should be relevant to the advertising objectives.
2. In advance of each test, researchers should agree on how the results will be used.
3. Multiple measures should be used.
4. The test should be based on some theory or model of human response to communication.
5. The testing procedure should allow for more than one exposure to the advertisement, if necessary.
6. In selecting alternate advertisements to include in the test, each should be at the same stage in the process as the test ad.
7. The test should provide controls to avoid biases.
8. The sample used for the test should be representative of the target sample.
9. The testing procedure should demonstrate reliability and validity.

Many advertisers and advertising agencies use the PACT principles. When they are followed, the likelihood increases dramatically that an advertising piece is being assessed effectively.

POSITIONING STRATEGY

Positioning is the process of creating a perception in the mind of consumers concerning the nature of a brand relative to the competition. A product can be positioned using approaches that feature the item's attributes, competitors, use or application, price-quality relationship, product user, product class, or a cultural symbol. Positioning is created by variables such as the quality of products, prices charged, methods of distribution, image, and other factors.

Two important principles underlie the positioning strategy. The first principle is that positioning is established by the relationship of a product and brand relative to competitors. Second, positioning is a perception in the minds of consumers. Consumers ultimately determine the position of a firm's products.

To effectively establish a brand's position, an advertising message must either reinforce what consumers already believe about a brand or move the consumer toward a more desirable evaluation of the brand. The goal of positioning advertising is to create a niche in a consumer's mind that a brand can occupy. Holding a niche position is important so consumers view a brand as being superior in some way to the competition. For example, Crest is positioned on its attribute of being the "best" toothpaste to fight cavities. As result, when consumers think of a toothpaste that effectively fights cavities, Crest is normally among the first brands to be considered.

POSTPURCHASE EVALUATION

The final step in the consumer decision-making process is the postpurchase evaluation phase. During this stage, the consumer evaluates a recently completed purchase. This review involves a comparison of what was expected from the product with what actually occurred. If the product meets expectations, the shopper is satisfied. If the product does not meet expectations, the individual experiences dissatisfaction.

The postpurchase evaluation affects future behavior of the consumer or business. Satisfaction normally creates additional purchases and positive word-of-mouth communications. Dissatisfaction normally leads to brand switching and negative word-of-mouth communications. The extent of repeat purchasing or brand switching depends on the strength of the satisfaction or dissatisfaction assessment. A mildly positive purchasing experience may not lead to more purchases and positive communications with family members and friends. A strongly positive experience, however, is much more likely to induce future purchases and positive comments to others. Also, a highly negative experience usually results in the consumer telling others about it, while a mildly negative experience may not result in any word-of-mouth communications.

Advertisers can affect postpurchase evaluations through reassurances at the time of the purchase. A car buyer who is told, following the purchase, that he or she made an excellent choice may have a level of reassurance that affects future feelings about the car, the company, and the salesperson. Also, follow-up in the case of negative experience may lessen its impact. Thus, a bad meal at a restaurant that results in the manager giving the customer the meal for free may result in fewer negative comments to others.

PRE- AND POSTTEST ANALYSIS

In evaluating advertisements or advertising campaigns, a common method of inquiry involves conducting both a pretest and a posttest. These tests allow the researcher to measure the change that occurs after the message or campaign has been seen. For example, when the objective of an advertising campaign is to increase brand awareness, it is important to measure the level of brand awareness prior to the launch of the ad campaign as well as immediately following its completion. If advance measures are not taken, it is much more difficult to evaluate the effectiveness of the campaign. Some advertisers measure brand awareness during the campaign to see if the advertisement is effective or if changes need to be made as the campaign progresses.

Pre- and posttest formats are used for a variety of purposes, including assessing ads as they are being prepared. In each case, the idea is to eliminate additional explanations for a change in a consumer's attitude or behavior. Thus, if one subject views a television ad in a hot and crowded theater, that individual may have a different reaction than a subject encountering the same ad in an uncrowded, air-conditioned space. To ensure effective assessments, it is important to control as many of these extraneous influences as possible.

PREEMPTIVE MESSAGE STRATEGY

A message strategy is the primary tactic used in the creation of an advertising message. Message strategies can be divided into four categories: cognitive, affective, conative, and brand. The cognitive message strategies, in turn, can be divided into five subcategories: generic, preemptive, unique selling proposition, hyperbole, and comparative.

In an advertisement using a preemptive message strategy, the advertiser makes claims regarding superiority based on a specific attribute or benefit of the product. The concept behind the preemptive strategy is that once a claim is made, it normally preempts the competition from making such a statement. For example, when a toothpaste becomes known as "the cavity fighter," the message and brand preempt other companies from making similar claims, even though all toothpastes fight cavities. Thus, when using a preemptive strategy, the key is to be the first company to state the advantage, thereby preempting the competition from saying it. Those who do are viewed as "me-too" brands or copycats. It is important to make certain that the advantage is real, identifiable, and can be proven.

PREMIUM

Premiums are prizes, gifts, or other special offers consumers receive when purchasing products. When a premium is offered, the consumer pays full price for the good or service. For example, a customer may purchase a full tank of gas and receive a car wash as the premium. The goal of a premium campaign is to add value to the product by offering a complementary item or something that has unique value to consumers.

Premiums can be used to enhance a brand's image as well as to boost sales. Premiums are a valuable consumer promotional tool, with over $4.5 billion per year being spent on them in the United States alone.[33] It is important to match the nature of the gift or prize with the product being offered, brand, and overall message portrayed by the company in its advertising and promotional messages.

PRICE-QUALITY RELATIONSHIP POSITIONING STRATEGY

Positioning is the process of creating a perception in the minds of consumers concerning the nature of a brand relative to the competition. Possible positioning approaches include attributes, competitors, use or application, price-quality, product user, product class, and cultural symbol.

There are three possible expressions of a price-quality relationship. The first two involve price-quality relationships on the extremes of the price range. At the top end, businesses will emphasize high quality, while at the bottom end low prices are emphasized. Therefore, consumers may believe Hallmark cards cost more, but are for those who "want to send the very best." Other firms seek to be a "low price leader," with no corresponding statement about quality. In the middle range are price-quality messages that suggest the most value for the dollar. Advertising messages in this vein suggest "high quality at a reasonable price." The critical ingredient in each of the three positions, highest price and quality, lowest price, or high quality at a reasonable price, is to match the position with the nature of the product as well as all other marketing messages.

PRIVATE BRAND

Private brands, also known as private labels, are proprietary brands marketed by an organization and normally distributed exclusively within the organization's outlets. Over the past fifty years, private brands have been on a roller coaster ride in terms of popularity and sales. To many individuals, private brands carry the connotation of lower price and inferior quality. Historically, the primary audience for private labels was individuals who were price sensitive. Not surprisingly, during recessions private labels often experience a growth in sales.

Over the past few years, private labels have changed in several ways. First, the quality of private-label products has improved. In some cases, the quality is perceived to be equal to or better than that of national brands. Second, although private labels still tend to be priced around 25 percent lower than national brands, some private labels are priced higher. These higher prices are due to a perceived increase in product quality.

Third, while loyalty toward many retail stores continues to grow, loyalty toward individual brands has been declining. Many shoppers visit specific stores rather than going to outlets selling specific brands. The customers are willing to buy the brands offered by their favorite store. This increase in store loyalty has led many department store managers to expand offerings of private brands. Often, store displays of private brands are now as prominent and attractive as national brands.

The fourth change in private labeling is in the area of advertising. Many firms now advertise private labels and brands. Although most of this advertising is created within the scope of store promotions, some advertising is being designed apart from stores. The purpose is to establish the private label name as a bona fide brand that can effectively compete with national products. The challenge to advertisers is to create perceptions of quality in private brands. Also, the goal is often to tie the private brand to a retail store.

PROBLEM RECOGNITION

Problem recognition is the first step in the consumer buying decision-making process. The consumer recognizes that a problem is present when a desired state is different than an actual state. As a result, the consumer has identified a want or need. For instance, after a long day at work, a female consumer might see her friend out enjoying a date. The friend is wearing a beautiful new dress. The consumer is currently not dating anyone. She may conclude that this state is different than her desired state. The consumer has identified a problem, which may be rectified by shopping for new clothes, finding new ways to circulate socially, or through some other course of action. The same consumer may see the same event and conclude that she is happy with her life as it is. Hence, no problem recognition is present.

Recognition of a problem is not always a cognitive event. A person may or may not actively think about a need yet still experience that need. For example, seeing and smelling cookies while walking past a bakery may trigger a reflex or desire to have them (a want). The consumer will then move to satisfy the need or want. Once a problem has been recognized, the consumer moves on to other stages in the buying decision-making process. This includes searching for information and purchasing alternatives. (*See* CONSUMER DECISION-MAKING PROCESS *for additional information.*)

PRODUCT CLASS POSITIONING STRATEGY

Positioning is the process of creating a perception in the minds of consumers concerning the nature of a brand relative to the competition. A product can be positioned using approaches that feature the item's attributes, competitors, use or application, price-quality relationship, product user, product class, or a cultural symbol. Position is created by variables such as the quality of products, prices charged, methods of distribution, image, and other factors.

One method used to position a product is based on the product's class. The class can be narrowly defined or viewed from a broader perspective. For example, orange juice may be viewed as part of the product class of breakfast drinks. Years ago, however, those in the orange juice-producing states created advertisements that were designed to position orange juice in a more general product beverage class. Advertising slogans such as "it's not just for breakfast anymore" were used to reposition orange juice as a product that may be consumed anytime during the day. This move repositioned orange juice as a healthy drink that can be served with or as a snack. While this generalized the product class, it also opened orange juice to compete with a greater number of beverages, including cranberry juice and other fruit juices as well as soft drinks.

PRODUCT USER POSITIONING STRATEGY

Positioning is the process of creating a perception in the minds of consumers concerning the nature of a brand relative to the competition. A product can be positioned using approaches that feature the item's attributes, competitors, use or application, price-quality relationship, product user, product class, or a cultural symbol. Position is created by variables such as the quality of products, prices charged, methods of distribution, image, and other factors.

A product user positioning strategy distinguishes a brand or product by clearly specifying who might use it. Magazines are often positioned by readership. Luxury automobiles are targeted to wealthy individuals. Internet fantasy sports leagues are targeted to sports fans that play them. The goal of specifying a product user strategy is to help the advertising team understand user characteristics. Messages can then be structured to move these buyers to action.

PROMOTIONAL MESSAGE STRATEGY

A message strategy is the primary tactic used in the creation of an advertising message. Message strategies can be divided into four categories: cognitive, affective, conative, and brand. Conative message strategies are designed to lead consumers to some type of behavior. The goal is to inspire an act or activity as opposed to a change in attitude.

Promotional message strategies are a subcategory of conative message strategies. The goal of a promotional message strategy is to support other promotional efforts, such as coupons, premiums, sweepstakes, or contests, by moving the consumer to action. Promotional message strategies are used in the business-to-business sector to support trade promotions and in the consumer sector to support consumer promotions. The goal is the same for both sectors: to inspire potential buyers to make a purchase or perform some activity. (*See* CONATIVE MESSAGE STRATEGY *for additional information.*)

PSYCHOGALVANOMETER

Advertisers are often interested in eliciting emotional responses to advertisements. Physiological arousal tests measure the fluctuations in a person's body functions that are associated with changing emotions. The most common types of physiological arousal tests are conducted using a psychogalvanometer, a pupillometric test, or a voice-pitch analysis.

A psychogalvanometer measures a person's perspiration levels. The psychogalvanometer works by evaluating the amount of perspiration located in the palm and fingers. A very fine electric current is sent through one finger and returns to the galvanometer through another finger. When an individual has an emotional reaction to a situation or advertisement, the amount of perspiration shed by the person normally changes.

The principle behind a psychogalvanometer is that arousal indicates a person is interested and involved emotionally. An advertisement producing these effects may be more memorable and powerful than one that is boring or receives no emotional response. A benefit of the psychogalvanometer is that it can be used to assess emotional reactions to many types of advertising communication pieces including television commercials, print ads, and radio ads.

PSYCHOGRAPHICS

Psychographics represent consumer attitudes, interests, and opinions (AIO). These mental characteristics provide advertisers with a wealth of information about consumers. By understanding these attitudes, interests, and opinions, advertising creatives are able to design ads that are appealing to select groups. When AIO measures are combined with demographic information, advertisers have a more complete understanding of the ad's target market. Identifying psychographic market segments helps the marketing team work toward the goal of matching what the firm does best with the most likely customers. (*See* MARKET SEGMENTATION *for additional information.*)

PUBLIC RELATIONS

The public relations (PR) department is a unit of a company assigned to manage publicity and other communications with outside agencies and groups. Public relations management is the process of developing positive messages about the company and reducing the impact of negative events, stories, and complaints that the company encounters.

Many aspects of PR are similar to those performed by the advertising department; however, the PR department plays a different role within an organization. Public relations teams focus on messages directed to a variety of internal and external stakeholders including employees, stockholders, public interest groups, the government, and society as a whole. PR has three key functions:

1. Monitoring internal and external publics
2. Providing positive information to each public that reinforces the integrated marketing plan and advertising direction
3. Reacting quickly to any shift in the position of any of the publics from the desired position

In addition to sending communications to each of the stakeholders, the PR department closely monitors the actions and opinions of individual groups. Changes in attitudes and views as well as messages from groups that raise concerns about the company are of vital interest to the PR department. It is the duty of the PR department to address these problems. Most important, it is the responsibility of the PR department to be certain that all forms of communication to each of these publics remain consistent with the firm's advertising plan along with the image the firm seeks to project.

PUFFERY

Puffery exists when a firm makes an exaggerated claim about its goods or services, without making an overt attempt to deceive or mislead. In advertising, some of the terms that are routinely utilized include "best," "greatest," and "finest." It is legally acceptable to claim that a company's tacos are the best in town. Courts and regulatory agencies such as the Federal Trade Commission view these statements as puffery and believe that consumers expect firms to routinely use them in their advertisements. An advertisement becomes false or deceptive only when a claim is made, for example, that a company's tacos contain more meat than the competitor's, when indeed they do not. Such a statement would be difficult to disprove. It would probably lead to objections by the competition. (*See* FEDERAL TRADE COMMISSION *for additional information.*)

PULSATING SCHEDULE OF ADVERTISING

A principle of effective advertising is to identify the appropriate length for an advertising campaign. Using the same advertisement over a longer period of time helps embed the message in long-term memory. At the same time, an ad campaign that runs too long causes viewers to become bored, lose interest, and finally to ignore the ad.

A pulsating advertising campaign schedule involves a continuous ad campaign with bursts of higher intensity (more ads in more media) during specific times of the year, most notably during peak seasons. For example, a retailer may run weekly ads in the newspaper all throughout the year, but during special times of the year, such as Christmas, may run three ads per week or may add television or radio to the media mix. (*See* CAMPAIGN DURATION *for additional information.*)

PUPILLOMETRIC METER

Advertisers are often interested in eliciting emotional responses to advertisements. Physiological arousal tests measure the fluctuations in a person's body functions that are associated with changing emotions. The most common types of physiological arousal tests are conducted using a psychogalvanometer, a pupillometric test, or a voice-pitch analysis.

A pupillometric meter is designed to measure pupil dilation. Dilation levels change with emotional arousal. Someone who is frightened has pupils that open wider. The same result occurs when a person is excited. Pupil dilation can be observed while the subject views a television or print advertisement. The belief is that when pupils dilate the subject is experiencing a positive reaction to the ad or marketing communication. Conversely, the same subject's pupils will become smaller when the reaction is negative. When conducting a pupillometric test, the subject's head must be held in a fixed position. This is so that the dilation of the pupil can then be measured throughout the ad. The idea is to measure each aspect of the message for both positive and negative responses. A graph can be superimposed on the commercial to show evaluators how each person responded to the advertisement.

PURCHASE DECISION

The fourth step in the consumer decision-making process is the purchase decision. It follows problem recognition, information search, and the evaluation of alternatives. When making a purchase decision, most of the time the consumer buys the brand chosen during the evaluation of alternatives stage. Often these evaluations occur at a retail store, and the purchase decision immediately follows the evaluation. Occasionally a consumer makes a different purchase decision than the one arrived at during the evaluation of alternatives. There are several possible reasons for a shift away from the evaluation process:

- A temporary change in the consumer's situation
- A desire for variety
- An impulse purchase
- An advertisement, consumer promotion, or some other marketing material
- The influence of a friend or relative

However, the most common outcome is to simply confirm the evaluation of alternatives by making the purchase choice that has already been decided. At that point, the salesperson will finalize the purchase by completing all paperwork, such as credit forms, and presenting the product to the buyer. (*See* CONSUMER DECISION-MAKING PROCESS *for additional information.*)

RADIO ADVERTISING

Radio has long been a traditional venue for advertising. Radio stations tend to have definable target markets based on specific formats, such as talk radio, lite mix rock music, oldies stations, religious programs, and others. A firm or advertising company can identify similar stations across the country.

Radio offers several advantages to advertisers. Through creative writing, powerful images can be inspired. Sound effects and memorable tunes assist in creating recall. Repetition also assists in recall.

Radio stations offer flexibility and a short lead time to prepare ads. Ads can also be changed quickly, which is helpful in volatile markets or in the retail sector. Radio makes it possible for a national company to modify an advertisement to fit local conditions. Modifications can be as simple as providing an address, a phone number, or Web address for each local outlet.

Radio offers intimacy. Listeners can develop a closeness to DJs and radio personalities that grows over time. The listener can even have a conversation with the DJ during a contest or when requesting a song or phoning in on a talk radio program. The bond or intimacy level means the radio personality has a higher level of credibility which gives an edge to products and services endorsed by the radio celebrity.

Radio is mobile. People carry radios to the beach, to the ballpark, to work, and to picnics. They listen at home, at work, and on the road in between. No other medium stays with the audience quite like radio.

Radio advertising is a low-cost option for a local firm. Ads can be placed at ideal times and adapted to local conditions. The key to radio is careful selection of stations, times, and construction of the ad. Immediate response techniques, contest entries, and other devices provide evidence of whether customers heard and responded to ads. Radio remotes, when the station broadcasts from a business location, have been popular methods of attracting attention to a new business (restaurants, service operations, small retail shops, etc.) or to a company seeking to make a major push for immediate customers.

For national advertisers, covering a large area with radio advertisements is challenging. To place a national advertisement requires contacting a large number of stations, networks, and companies.

For business-to-business advertisers, radio provides the opportunity to reach businesses during working hours, since many employees listen to the radio during office hours. Radio reaches business people while in transit to or from work.

RATINGS

Ratings are a measure of the percentage of a target market that is exposed to a television show or article in a print medium. The most common ratings are produced by Nielsen Media Research. Nielsen ratings indicate the percentage of households within the United States that are tuned to a particular television show. One rating point is equivalent to 1 percent of the households with televisions, or approximately 1,055,000 households. This is based on the estimate of 105.5 million television households in the United States.

A television show with a Nielsen rating of 20.3 has 20.3 percent of the households at that given hour (e.g., 9:00 p.m.) on the given night (e.g., Wednesday) tuned into that particular program. The Nielsen rating of 20.3 translates into approximately 21,416,000 households (1,055,000 × 20.3). If, on the same night the Nielsen rating for another program was 10.8, the rating would indicate that another 10.8 percent of U.S. households were watching that program.

RATIONAL APPEAL

The type of appeal of an advertisement is the general tone and nature of the commercial or message. The appeal is chosen after a review of a creative brief and the objective of the advertisement. There are seven primary appeals:

1. Fear
2. Humor
3. Sex

4. Music
5. Rationality
6. Emotions
7. Scarcity

When a rational appeal is used, consumers are expected to use reason and thought processes when making purchase decisions. A rational appeal provides the information needed to help make a high-quality, reasonable decision. A rational appeal is often designed to follow the hierarchy of effects stages of awareness, knowledge, liking, preference, conviction, and purchase. Ads are designed for one of the six steps. For example, in the knowledge stage, the advertisement transmits basic information. In the preference stage, the ad shifts to presenting logical reasons why one particular brand is superior. A rational ad should lead to a stronger conviction about a product's benefits, so that eventually the purchase is made.

To be successful, rational appeals rely on consumers actively processing the information presented in an advertisement. Messages that are consistent with current concepts or beliefs are the most effective. New messages or information must be linked to current memory information to be retained. New information is therefore more difficult to present.

Print media offer the best outlets for rational appeals. Print advertisements allow readers greater opportunities to process copy information. The reader can pause and take time to read the written content. Television and radio commercials are short, which makes it more difficult for viewers to process message arguments.

Rational appeals are often used to advertise high-involvement and complex products. High-involvement decisions require considerable cognitive activity, and consumers spend more time evaluating the attributes of the individual brands. Rational appeals work well in those settings. In terms of cognitive activity, a rational appeal can easily be designed to develop or change attitudes. This tactic is most effective when a consumer has a particular interest in the product or brand being advertised.

Rational appeals are not the most effective in terms of attracting attention to an advertisement. In fact, rational appeals tend to have the lowest attraction of all of the appeals and also tend to have very low intrusive capabilities. (*See* HIERARCHY OF EFFECTS MODEL *for additional information.*)

REACH

Reach is a number that represents people, households, or businesses in a target audience exposed to a media vehicle or message schedule at least once during a given period. A typical period is four weeks. The number represents the buyers that an ad reached. For instance, for a company selling Western apparel, the advertiser would seek to know the reach of each country and western radio station in a target market area.

Reach is also important in the business-to-business sector. An advertising agency will try to identify, for example, the reach of ad in *Business Week* as it pertains to members of buying centers for individual products, such as financial services for a business.

Reach information is more helpful when it is combined with frequency numbers. It is also important to consider effective frequency and effective reach. Effective reach refers to the number of individuals that must be exposed to an advertisement for it to be effective, and effective frequency refers to the number of times an individual must be exposed to an advertisement for it to be effective. (*See* EFFECTIVE FREQUENCY AND EFFECTIVE REACH *and* FREQUENCY *for additional information.*)

REACTION TEST

A reaction test is a method of evaluating advertisements. It is a subcategory of concept testing. The purpose of a reaction test is to determine consumer feelings about an advertisement or an advertising campaign, most notably whether the feelings are negative or positive. Many advertising agencies use focus groups for this purpose, especially during the design stage. If the focus group reacts negatively to an ad or particular copy in an ad, the agency makes changes before the ad is launched. It must be kept in mind, however, that an advertisement can receive negative reactions.

It is important to recognize that an advertisement that receives negative reactions can damage a product's image. A primary advantage of reaction tests is that they allows researchers to explore negative feelings. Information gathered can provide creatives with input on how to modify the ad to make it more acceptable. (*See* CONCEPT TESTING *for additional information.*)

RECALL TEST

Recall tests are a popular method of evaluating advertising because consumer recall of a brand and the corresponding message are vital elements in the success of a marketing campaign. Recall tests involve asking individuals to recall what ads they viewed in a given setting or time period. Then, in progressive steps, the subjects are asked to identify information about the ad. Some of the parts of an advertisement that can be tested for recall include

- product name or brand,
- firm name,
- company location,
- theme music,
- spokesperson,
- tagline,
- incentive being offered,
- product attributes, and
- primary selling point of the advertisement.

A day-after recall (DAR) test is one common form of recall testing, particularly television advertisements. Normally, DAR tests use unaided recall in which subjects are asked to name, or recall, the ads they saw or heard the previous evening, without being given any prompts or memory jogs.

There are two approaches to recall testing for print media, such as magazines and newspapers. In the first, consumers are contacted the day after the ad appeared. The individuals name the ads they recall and then are asked a series of questions to discover the features of the advertisement they remember. In the second, an individual is given a magazine for a certain period of time (normally one week) and instructed to read it as he or she normally would during leisure time. Then the researcher returns and asks a series of questions about which ads were memorable and what features the individual could re-member. In the business-to-business sector, the second method is a popular way to test ads for trade journals. A company or advertise-ment that is recalled has become part of the consumer's evoked set.[34]

A second type of recall test is the aided recall method. Aided recall tests use prompts for consumers, who are told the product category and, if necessary, names of specific brands as part of the test. The re-spondent still does not know which brand or ad is being studied. When the consumer states that he or she does recall seeing a specific brand being advertised, the person is then asked to provide as many details as possible about the ad. At that point, no further clues are given regarding the content of the ad.

In both aided and unaided recall tests, when incorrect information is provided the researcher continues the questioning. Subjects are never told they have given inaccurate answers. Such responses are important data. Memory is not perfect in either aided or unaided re-call situations. Subjects may mention commercials that did not actu-ally appear during the test period but rather were viewed at some other time. Although this may seem strange, bear in mind that the av-erage person sees between 50 and 100 ads on a typical night of televi-sion viewing. It is easy to become confused.

Recall tests are used primarily after ads are aired or have been shown in print. They can also be used in the early stages of communi-cation development. In these instances, the study uses a more stan-dard experimental design. For example, an advertising agency that has created a new business-to-business ad may wonder if the ad would work when aired with consumer ads. Using a theater lab set-ting, the new ad can be placed in a documentary with other ads. At the end, either the aided or unaided recall method can be used to measure ad and brand awareness. (*See* EVOKED SET *and* RECOGNITION TEST *for additional information.*)

RECEIVER

In most communication models, a sender conveys a message to the receiver or a set of receivers. The receiver is the intended audience. Effective advertising communication occurs when customers (the receivers) decode or understand the message as it was intended when it was encoded by the sender.

RECENCY THEORY

Recency theory is based on the idea that a consumer's attention is selective and is focused on his or her individual needs and wants. The theory suggests that consumers use selective attention processes to consider advertisements. Attention is focused on messages that meet a person's needs or wants. The closer in time an advertisement is to a purchase, either past or future, the more powerful the ad will be, and it is more likely the consumer will pay attention and respond favorably to the ad.

Recency theory postulates that advertising is a waste of money when a message reaches an individual who is not in the market for a particular product or does not need the product. Therefore, careful attention must be given to targeting advertisements to consumers with wants or needs that are met by a firm's goods and services.

Advertisers who subscribe to recency theory believe that one ad exposure is sufficient to influence a consumer when that person or business needs the product being promoted. Additional exposures may actually be a waste of money. The difficulty, however, with recency theory is finding that particular moment when the consumer or business is in the market for the product. Since each consumer or business may need or want a particular product at different times, ads must run on a regular basis to ensure that they will be seen within an acceptable time range. (*See* THREE-EXPOSURE HYPOTHESIS *for an alternative view.*)

RECOGNITION TEST

A recognition test is an advertising message evaluation methodology. The purpose of message evaluations is to determine if advertisements have the desired effect on the intended audience. Evaluation or testing of advertising communications can occur at any stage of development.

During recognition tests, individuals are given copies of an advertisement and asked if they recognize it or have seen it before. Those who say they have seen the ad are asked to provide additional details about when and where the ad was encountered (e.g., specific television program, name of the magazine, location of the billboard, etc.), to make sure the ad was actually seen. These details will also provide information as to the best locations and media.

Next, the individual is asked a series of questions about the advertisement to gather information and insights into consumer attitudes and reactions to the ad. Recognition tests help when the advertiser is concerned about perceptions of the advertisement. This is especially important for ads using a cognitive message strategy or situations in which some type of reasoning process is invoked in persuading the consumer of the value of a product.

Recall and recognition tests are often used together. Recognition tests tend to measure how many people saw an advertisement, while recall tests tend to measure how many saw the ad and were also sufficiently interested to take the time to actually view or read the ad and incorporate it into their memory.

Many ingredients affect the degree of recognition of an ad. For example, in print media, a larger advertisement has a greater impact than a small ad. The larger the ad, the higher the level of recognition. Also, when the consumer uses the brand being displayed in an advertisement, the likelihood of recognizing the ad rises. Similar results occur when a test is used to determine if the ad is liked or deemed interesting. An ad that a person likes is about 75 percent more likely to be recognized than an ad the individual did not like. This is one reason celebrities are often selected for ads. If an individual likes the celebrity in the advertisement, he or she will be more likely to recognize the ad. For ads the respondent thought was interesting, the odds of recognition were about 50 percent higher than for ads that were not deemed interesting. (*See* MESSAGE EVALUATION *and* RECALL TEST *for additional information.*)

RESONANCE MESSAGE STRATEGY

A message strategy is the primary tactic used in the creation of an advertising message. Message strategies can be divided into four categories: cognitive, affective, conative, and brand. The affective message strategies, in turn, can be divided into two subcategories: resonance and emotional.

A resonance strategy is a type of affective message strategy in which an advertisement is designed to connect a product with a consumer's experiences to develop stronger ties between the product and the consumer. For example, using music from the 1960s is designed to take baby boomers back to that time and the pleasant experiences they had growing up. Any strongly held memory or emotional attachment is a candidate for resonance advertising.

Many emotions resonate with consumers including love, affection, feelings of attachment to one's family, happiness, trust, and others. The goal of resonance advertisement is to connect one of these positive emotions to a brand, product, or company.

SALES PROMOTION

See CONSUMER PROMOTION.

SALES-RESPONSE FUNCTION CURVE

A sales-response function curve is an S-shaped curve that depicts the impact of advertising expenditures on sales. Typically, sales are low with a small amount of advertising because of low awareness and lack of persuasive advertising. As advertising expenditures increase, there is a threshold at which sales begin to climb rapidly. It is at this threshold that advertising expenditures are optimized. As advertising dollars continue to increase, the impact on sales begins to diminish and even flatten out. At that point, adding more money to the advertising budget does not increase sales substantially because the market is already saturated with the firm's advertising.

The key to effective use of the sales-response function curve is finding that level of advertising expenditures that will generate the optimal level of sales. Too little spent on advertising will not impact sales enough and too much spending will cause diminishing returns. (*See* CARRYOVER EFFECTS; DECAY EFFECTS; *and* THRESHOLD EFFECT *for additional information.*)

SCARCITY APPEAL

The appeal of an advertisement is the general tone and nature of the commercial or message. The appeal is chosen after a review of a creative brief and the objective of the advertisement. The seven major types of appeals are

1. fear,
2. humor,
3. sex,
4. music,
5. rationality,
6. emotions, and
7. scarcity.

Scarcity appeals urge consumers to buy a particular product because of a limitation. In most situations, when a limited supply of a product exists, the value of that product increases. The limitation can be in the number of products available or, more often, that the product is available for only a limited time. For example, at the turn of the century, General Mills introduced a Cheerios line called Millenios as a limited-time product. Tiny 2s were added to the familiar O-shaped cereal Cheerios.[35] The scarcity concept is also used for musical compilations encouraging consumers to buy the product because it is available for only a limited time. By making sure it is not available in retail stores, marketers increase its scarcity value.

The scarcity appeal is often used with other promotional tools. A manufacturer may advertise a limited price discount offer to retailers who stock up early for Christmas or some other holiday season. Contests and sweepstakes also run for limited times.

SEGMENTATION BY AGE

A market segment is a set of businesses or group of individual consumers with distinct characteristics. Market segmentation is the process of locating and dividing the market into specific groups based on their needs, attitudes, and interests.

One common method of segmentation is to identify consumers by age. Children, teenagers, young adults, older adults, and senior citizens are all targeted by different advertising approaches. Often age-related factors are combined with other demographics such as gender or race to create a smaller, more homogeneous group. Simply targeting by age may not be precise enough to develop effective advertising strategies. For example, older women may be primary targets for certain age-specific products. Working women with families may be targeted with ads for conveniences, such as ready-made foods and snacks, and quick-lube oil change facilities.

Children have become a significant market segment. Not only do they have discretionary income of their own to spend, they are also a major impact on their parents' purchase decisions. Appeals to children will often tie a product or toy to a popular television character.

Another growing age-based demographic group is seniors, defined as individuals over the age of fifty-five. In the past, all seniors were treated as one market and tended to be stereotyped in ads. Often they were pictured as elderly grandparents or as feeble but avid gardeners. Several firms discovered that many seniors lead active lives and many are not gardeners. (*See* MARKET SEGMENTATION *for additional information.*)

SEGMENTATION BY ETHNIC HERITAGE

A market segment is a set of businesses or group of individual consumers with distinct characteristics. Market segmentation is the process of locating and dividing the market into specific groups based on their needs, attitudes, and interests.

Segmentation of consumer markets by ethnicity is a common approach. Three of the largest ethnic groups in the United States are African Americans, Hispanics, and Asian Americans. African-American economic power exceeds $400 billion annually, while Hispanic sector purchases are in excess of $300 billion. Often each ethnic group is further segmented into subgroups. For instance, the Hispanic community is made up of individuals from Latin America, Mexico, Cuba, and Puerto Rico. The Asian community includes individuals of Korean, Japanese, Filipino, Vietnamese, and Chinese descent.

In addition to the three larger ethnic groups, a substantial number of immigrants from India and Pakistan have recently arrived in the United States. Another large group is coming from the Middle East and eastern European countries. Each ethnic group contains multiple subgroups.

Although different in many ways, these ethnic groups have several common threads. All tend to be more brand loyal than their white counterparts. Members of these groups value quality and are willing to pay a higher price for quality and brand identity. They value relationships with companies and are loyal to the companies that make the effort to establish a connection with them.

Ethnic advertising requires more than expenditures on ethnically owned radio stations or advertising agencies. It requires an understanding of various ethnic groups and writing marketing communications that speak to their cultures and values. To advertise effectively to ethnic groups, it is important to develop new creative approaches that respect America's ethnic differences while also highlighting its similarities, which means a careful study of the subtleties of multiculturalism. Indications are strong that ethnic consumers reward companies that invest in them. In addition to advertising, becoming involved in ethnic community groups and civic and trade associations is beneficial.

SEGMENTATION BY GENDER

A market segment is a set of businesses or group of individual consumers with distinct characteristics. Market segmentation is the process of locating and dividing the market into specific groups based on their needs, attitudes, and interests.

Using gender is a common method of segmentation. Males and females purchase different products, buy products that are similar but that have different features (e.g., deodorants for women versus men), and buy the same products for dissimilar reasons (stereos, televisions).

Many advertisements are targeted toward females. Women are a major market, especially as the number of women working has risen. Nearly 70 percent of the women in the workforce express concerns about being able to balance work and family. This concern changes the ways many companies market products to women. Goods and services that offer convenience, flexibility, and independence are in demand. Advertisements featuring these advantages are often successful. Many working women also enjoy rewarding themselves. This leads to purchases of CDs, dining out, and other perks as well as the use of services such as health spas and beauty salons.[36]

Traditionally, men have been the target for major products such as automobiles as well as sporting events and sports products. But in recent years, advertisers have come to realize that men also purchase groceries, laundry detergents, and products that in the past were purchased primarily by females. Advertising these types of products to men requires a different approach.

SEGMENTATION BY GENERATION

A market segment is a set of businesses or group of individual consumers with distinct characteristics. Market segmentation is the process of locating and dividing the market into specific groups based on their needs, attitudes, and interests.

One method of segmentation for consumer markets is by generation. The concept behind this method of segmentation is that common experiences and events create bonds between people beyond those based merely on age. Based on this idea, seven cohorts or generations have been identified:[37]

1. Depression cohort (born 1912-1921)
2. World War II cohort (born 1922-1927)
3. Postwar cohort (born 1928-1945)
4. Boomers I cohort (born 1946-1954)

5. Boomers II cohort (born 1955-1965)
6. Generation X cohort (born 1966-1976)
7. Generation Y cohort (born 1977-1994)

People from each of these groups have experienced significant external events during their late adolescence or early adulthood years. Most recently, today's teenagers will distinctly remember the events of September 11, 2001. These events impact social values, attitudes, and preferences. Based on similar experiences, these cohorts of individuals develop common preferences for music and foods, as well as other products. They also tend to respond to the same types of advertising appeals.

SEGMENTATION BY GEOGRAPHIC AREA

A market segment is a set of businesses or group of individual consumers with distinct characteristics. Market segmentation is the process of locating and dividing the market into specific groups based on their needs, attitudes, and interests.

One method of segmentation, in both business and consumer markets, is to identify a geographic area or region. Retailers who must limit advertising campaigns to specific areas often use this approach. Many companies conduct direct mail campaigns in specific geographic target areas. Geographic segmentation is normally reserved for more basic products (restaurants, foods) or items of specific interest to a region.

The primary disadvantage of geographic segmentation is that every member of the area is exposed to an advertisement, regardless of interest in the good or service. Using geographic segmentation alone does not allow a firm to focus on a more specific target market containing only those most likely to make purchases. However, when geographic information is combined with psychographic or other personal information, a more directed campaign can be prepared. (*See* GEODEMOGRAPHIC SEGMENTATION *for additional information.*)

SEGMENTATION BY INCOME

A market segment is a set of businesses or group of individual consumers with distinct characteristics. Market segmentation is the process of locating and dividing the market into specific groups based on their needs, attitudes, and interests.

A longstanding method of segmentation of consumer markets is by level of income. This is because spending is normally directed at three large categories of goods:

1. Necessities
2. Sundries
3. Luxuries

Lower levels of income mean consumers purchase mostly necessities, such as food, clothing, and other basic materials. As household income increases, it becomes possible to purchase more sundries, or the things that are nice to own but not necessary. Sundries include televisions, computers, CD players, and more fashionable clothes. Vacation spending is a type of sundry expenditure. Luxuries are items most people cannot afford, or can afford only once in a lifetime. High-income households purchase luxuries including yachts, expensive automobiles, extravagant vacation resorts, and other high-cost goods and services.

Marketers work closely with advertising creatives to prepare messages targeted to various income groups, and to select media that match those groups. An affective advertisement matches the product to the market and the medium selected.

SEGMENTATION BY INDUSTRY

A market segment is a set of businesses or group of individual consumers with distinct characteristics. Market segmentation is the process of locating and dividing the market into specific groups based on their needs, attitudes, and interests.

In business-to-business advertising, one method of segmentation is to identify markets by industry. Many firms use the NAICS (North America Industry Classification System) code to specify target markets. The NAICS code is replacing the SIC (Standard Industrial Classification) coding system. When studying industry-based market segments, each can be broken down into smaller subcomponents when necessary. For example, Ambulatory Health Care Services would include physicians, dentists, chiropractors, and optometrists. The NAICS divides the economy into twenty broad sectors instead of the ten used by the SIC system and uses a six-digit code rather than the SIC four-digit code. The six-digit code allows greater stratification of industries and provides greater flexibility in creating classifications. Corporate information and data are recorded with the federal government using the NAICS, making it a logical system to choose for purposes of identifying market segments.

Advertisements are created for companies within various industries and targeted to matching media, such as trade magazines. The goal is to maximize exposures to individuals who make the actual purchasing decisions for companies within a given industry.

SEGMENTATION BY PRODUCT USAGE

A market segment is a set of businesses or group of individual consumers with distinct characteristics. Market segmentation is the process of locating and dividing the market into specific groups based on their needs, attitudes, and interests.

One method of segmentation for both business and consumer markets is according to how a product is used. In business-to-business markets, numerous services have a variety of uses for distinct customers. For example, in the hotel industry, one major source of revenue is business events and conferences. A hotel or resort may segment the business market based on various types of events. Single-day seminars require only a meeting room and refreshments. A full conference generates rentals for meeting rooms and lodging, fees for banquets, and often traffic into a hotel's bar or lounge. Segmenting the market based on how the hotel's facilities and staff will be used allows the hotel's manager to prepare advertising materials that address the needs of each specific type of conference.

For consumer markets, products and services have specific uses for individual customers. For example, fitness centers often segment the market by product usage because some individuals use a fitness center to lose weight while others use the same facility for weight training. Still others join the center as a place to maintain good health or simply to socialize. By focusing on a particular segment of the fitness market, a business can better meet the needs of their market and develop a niche.

SEGMENTATION BY SIZE

A market segment is a set of businesses or group of individual consumers with distinct characteristics. Market segmentation is the process of locating and dividing the market into specific groups based on their needs, attitudes, and interests.

One method of segmentation for business markets is according to the size of client companies. Large firms have different needs than smaller companies and therefore should be contacted in a different manner. For instance, the marketing effort often focuses on the other company's purchasing department when the firm is large. For smaller firms, the owner or general manager is often the one making the purchase decisions.

A smaller firm's resources may not be sufficient to handle the demands of a large firm. For example, an advertising agency in St. Louis may decide to focus on small and medium-size businesses. They realize they do not have sufficient staff to handle large accounts. Another agency may feel the small-business market is neglected and focus entirely on small businesses.

SENDER

The sender is the starting point of a communication model. The sender is the person or advertiser attempting to deliver a message or idea. In advertising, senders are companies that manufacture and sell products or retailers who are promoting their store. Every company and every brand will try to garner the customer's attention and at some point be a sender of communication. In most cases, these firms hire advertising agencies to construct messages and choose an appropriate outlet.

SEVERITY

An advertising appeal that is based on fear must be sufficiently strong to attract the viewer's attention but not so powerful that the viewer turns away from the advertisement. A model that helps design fear appeals is called the behavioral response model. The goal of this model is to create an advertisement that relies on two elements, vulnerability and severity.

Severity is a calculation made by a viewer about how strong the negative consequences of an action will be. For example, an advertisement suggesting that smoking is bad for your health may outline heart attacks, strokes, and various forms of cancer as the consequences of smoking. Once a viewer or consumer believes the consequences are severe enough to be avoided, the individual will be more receptive to the other elements of the message. (*See* FEAR APPEAL *for additional information.*)

SEXUAL APPEAL

The appeal of an advertisement is the general tone and nature of the commercial or message. The appeal is chosen after a review of a creative brief and the objective of the advertisement. The seven major types of appeals are

1. fear,
2. humor,
3. sex,
4. music,
5. rationality,
6. emotions, and
7. scarcity.

The sexual appeal has been employed in advertising in five ways:

1. subliminal techniques,
2. nudity or partial nudity,
3. sexual suggestiveness,
4. overt sexuality, and
5. sensuality.

Subliminal approaches place sexual cues or icons in advertisements where they will affect a viewer's subconscious mind. Research has indicated, however, that subliminal cues are not really effective in impacting viewers. To be effective, the sexual cue or icon must be noticed, which means it ceases to be subliminal.[38] Although a few advertisers may place sexual cues or icons in an ad in a subliminal manner, they are peripheral to another type of appeal.

A large number of companies use nudity or partial nudity to sell their products. These ads are designed to elicit a sexual response from the viewer.[39] Both males and females may be nude or partially nude in ads and are effective in eliciting responses from viewers. Because nudity may offend some individuals, many advertisers try sexual suggestiveness. With this approach, the ad merely suggests sexuality through well-known cues, words, or actions of the models in the ad. At the other extreme is the use of overt, explicit sexuality, which is becoming more common in advertising. The trend is even more noticeable in Europe than in the United States. The amount of male/female physical, sexual contact in an advertisement has increased dramatically in the past fifty years.[40]

The final sex appeal approach is the use of sensuality. Such ads are often targeted toward women who might respond better to a sensual suggestion than to an overt sexual approach. Instead of strong sexual images, an alluring glance across a crowded room is shown. Sensuality is currently viewed as a more sophisticated sexual appeal that relies on the imagination. It portrays images of romance and love rather than raw sexuality.

Sexual appeals have been used by a number of advertisers to build brand awareness. A number of studies have investigated sex and nudity in advertising. Almost all of them conclude that sex and nudity do increase attention, regardless of the gender of the individuals in the advertisement or the gender of the audience. Although sexually oriented ads attract attention, brand recall for ads using a sexual appeal is lower than ads using some other type of appeal. Thus, it appears that although people watch the advertisement, the sexual theme distracts them from paying attention to the brand name.[41]

In addition to gaining attention, sexually oriented advertisements are rated as being more interesting to viewers. The paradox, however, is that although the controversial ads are more interesting, they fail to increase the transmission of information. Respondents could not remember any more about the message of the ad than individuals who viewed the same ad but without a controversial sexual theme.[42]

A common sexual appeal in advertising is to use decorative models. Decorative models are defined as models in an advertisement whose primary purpose is to adorn the product as a sexual or attractive stimulus. The model has no functional purpose except to attract attention. Still, automobile, tool, and beer commercials often use female models dressed in bikinis to stand by products. (*See* DECORATIVE MODEL *for additional information.*)

SIMILARITY

One common tactic of advertisers is to utilize a source or spokesperson with the characteristic of similarity. Consumers are inclined to be influenced when a message is delivered by a person who is similar in some way such as appearance, hobbies, interests, or attitude. Real person spokespersons and average-looking sources are most likely to exhibit the similarity characteristic. (*See* SOURCE CHARACTERISTICS *and* SPOKESPERSONS AND SOURCES *for additional information.*)

SLICE-OF-LIFE EXECUTION

Slice-of-life is a type of executional framework. Other types of executional frameworks include animation, dramatization, testimonials, authoritative, demonstration, fantasy, and informative. In slice-of-life commercials, advertisers provide solutions to everyday problems faced by consumers or businesses.

Slice-of-life executions rely on the common things people experience, especially problems they encounter. Goods or services are made available to solve those problems. The most common slice-of-life format has four components:

1. Encounter
2. Problem
3. Interaction
4. Solution

Actors are used to portray the dilemma or problem. Sometimes the actors solve the problems themselves. In others, a voice-over explains the benefits or solution to the problem that the good, service, or company provides.

The slice-of-life approach was introduced and made popular by Proctor & Gamble. During the 1980s, about 60 percent of all of P&G's advertisements used slice-of-life scenarios. Now the company has shifted to more humor, animation, and comparative types of executional frameworks. Still, the slice-of-life executional framework remains effective. Studies indicate that the slice-of-life format scores above average in its persuasion ability, which is important in leading consumers into changing their brand preferences.[43] Also, benefits can be presented in a positive light without making brazen or harsh claims and without directly disparaging the competition.[44]

Slice-of-life commercials are also used heavily in business-to-business advertisements. This executional framework is popular because it allows the advertiser to highlight how their product can meet business needs.

Slice-of-life executional frameworks are possible in most media, including magazines or billboards, since a single picture can depict a normal, everyday situation or problem. The secret is to let one image tell the entire story, with the product being the solution.

SOCIAL RESPONSIBILITY ADVERTISING

Social responsibility is the obligation of an organization to be ethical, accountable, and reactive to the needs of society. Companies engaged in socially responsible activities generate quality publicity and customer loyalty. These activities support the firm's brand as well as the company's advertising program.

A common approach to social responsibility is to attempt to tie beneficial activities to methods for attracting customers. This includes the following:

1. Identifying areas where a company can undertake a positive activity.
2. Making certain local media are made aware of these efforts to enhance the chances for positive publicity.
3. Informing employees so that they will tell family members, friends, and neighbors about these positive activities.
4. Investing in advertising that is designed to highlight company efforts. Company-friendly publicity and advertising efforts generate goodwill in the community.

Being socially responsible and marketing those efforts can help build an effective image for the firm.

Also, firms that work toward reducing unfair practices, pollution, harassment, and other negative activities are more likely to stay out of court and suffer fewer negative word-of-mouth comments by dissatisfied consumers.

In general, long-term prospects improve when company leaders take the time to identify areas in which their organizations can improve the lives of employees and members of the community. Two examples of altruistic marketing activities are cause-related marketing and green marketing. (*See* CAUSE-RELATED MARKETING *and* GREEN MARKETING *for additional information.*)

SOURCE CHARACTERISTICS

In an advertisement, the individual who speaks on behalf of the company is known as the source or spokesperson. One key ingredient in developing an effective advertisement is to select an appropriate spokesperson. In evaluating sources, most account executives and companies consider five major characteristics:

1. Attractiveness
2. Likeability
3. Trustworthiness
4. Expertise
5. Credibility

Attractiveness has two ingredients, physical attractiveness and personality characteristics. Physical attractiveness is usually an important asset for an endorser. Physically attractive spokespersons often create more favorable impressions. This is true for both male and female audiences. The attractiveness of the spokesperson's personality is also important. This personality component helps viewers form emotional bonds with the spokesperson.

Closely related to the personality component of attractiveness is likability. Consumers respond more positively to spokespersons they like. This liking has various sources. It may be that consumers liked a movie in which the person acted or the character played by the actor. An athlete who plays on the favorite team of the consumer gains likability. Other individuals are likable because they support the favorite charities of consumers.

Some spokespersons may be likable and attractive, but are not viewed as trustworthy. Trustworthiness is the degree of confidence or the level of acceptance consumers have for the spokesperson's message. A trustworthy spokesperson helps consumers believe the message. Likability and trustworthiness are related as people who are liked tend to be trusted and people who are disliked tend not to be trusted.

The fourth characteristic is expertise. Sources with higher levels of expertise are more believable than sources with low expertise. Often when expertise is desired in an ad, the ad agency may opt for the CEO or a trained or educated expert in the field.

The final source selection characteristic is credibility, which is the sum of all the characteristics. Thus, it is a composite of attractiveness, trustworthiness, likability, and expertise. Credibility affects a receiver's acceptance of the spokesperson and message. A credible source is one that is believable. Most sources will not score high on all four attributes, but will need to score high on at least two or three to be perceived as credible. One reason advertisers use celebrities so often is that they are more likely to possess at least an element of all the characteristics. A CEO, expert, or typical person is probably going to lack one or more of them.

SPECIALTY ADVERTISING

Specialty advertising consists of free gifts, such as pens, coffee mugs, calendars, and key chains, that are given to a company's customers. Normally, the company's name is imprinted on the specialty item, often along with a message, logo, or tagline. To be effective, these messages and taglines should be tied in with the advertising theme. These promotional gifts provide customers with a constant reminder of the company and serve to reinforce the firm's advertising.

Many specialty advertising gifts are distributed at trade shows by salespeople. Others are sent as part of direct mail campaigns. Companies spend almost $12 billion annually on promotional items [45] The concept behind a specialty gift is known as reciprocation, which is the human desire to return a gift or favor. In business, this psychological advantage can be used in a number of ways. At a trade show, promotional gifts can create a positive impression of the business. The gift must convey the intended message and create the desire to return the favor by examining the company's products and possibly making a purchase in the future.

To be effective, a specialty item should be unique. For example, at one trade show a cotton gin company gave away miniature bales of cotton with their logo printed on the bale. The item was not useful, but it was unique. In another setting, a florist gave a rose to each woman attending a Latino businesswomen's conference. Both gifts focused the customer's attention on the company's product.[46]

Specialty gifts may also be used to reinforce buying decisions to make a customer feel that a good choice was made. Gifts can strengthen business relationships and also can help stimulate interest from a new potential prospect.

SPOKESPERSONS AND SOURCES

In an advertisement, the individual who speaks on behalf of the company is known as the source, or spokesperson. A major issue in the development of an advertisement is the selection of the spokesperson. In some situations a source may not be used at all. If a spokesperson is to be used, then a creative has four alternatives:

1. Celebrities
2. CEOs
3. Experts
4. Typical persons

Approximately 20 percent of all advertisements utilize celebrity spokespersons. Payments to celebrities account for around 10 percent of all advertising dollars spent.[47] These endorsers are popular, because their stamp of approval on a product enhances the brand's image. Some celebrities create emotional bonds with the products. This bond is often more profound for younger consumers. Celebrities also establish the brand's "personality," if the brand's characteristics are effectively tied to the spokesperson. In developing a brand personality, the brand should already be established.

The second type of source is a CEO. A highly visible and personable CEO can become a major asset for the firm and its products. Many local companies succeed, in part, because their owners are out front in small-market television commercials. They can even begin to take on the status of local celebrities.

Expert sources include physicians, lawyers, accountants, and financial planners. These experts are not celebrities or CEOs. Instead, experts provide testimonials, serve as authoritative figures, demonstrate products, and enhance the credibility of an informative advertisement.

The final category of spokesperson is the typical-person source. There are two types. The first is a paid actor or model who portrays or resembles everyday people. The second is actual typical, everyday people who are used in advertisements. The "man-on-the-street" form of advertising uses typical persons. These sources are becoming more common. One reason for this is the overuse of celebrities. Many experts believe that consumers have become saturated with celebrity endorsers and that the positive impact today is not as strong as it was in the past.[48] (*For information on selection of spokespersons, see* SOURCE CHARACTERISTICS.)

SPONSORSHIP MARKETING

Sponsorship marketing programs involve a company paying money to sponsor someone or some group that is participating in an activity. For years, local firms sponsored everything from Little League baseball and soccer teams to adult bowling teams. Other organizations sponsor college scholarship programs, special "days" (such as a Labor Day festival), as well as individuals who enter various contests. Many local car race tracks feature drivers who are sponsored by various companies.

Sponsorships accomplish many different objectives for organizations. For example, sponsorships can

- enhance a company's image,
- increase the firm's visibility,
- differentiate a company from its competitors,
- showcase specific goods and services,
- help the firm develop closer relationships with current and prospective customers, and
- unload excess inventory.

In choosing a sponsorship, advertisers attempt to match the audience profile with the company's target market. Marketing executives also consider the image of the individual participant or group to make sure it relates to the firm's image. Normally the sponsoring firm will attempt to get an exclusive contract.

Many sponsorships are related to sports because of their popularity. In addition to the audience attending the game or competition, many more watch on television. The idea is to take the loyalty associated with an athlete and transfer part of it to the product or company.

Some organizations have moved away from sports sponsorships toward music and the arts, such as classical music groups and jazz bands, visual art exhibits by noted painters, dance troupes, and theater performances. Many of these philanthropic efforts are leveraged by having the name of the company strongly associated with the cultural activity. This includes printing the name of the firm on programs and regularly giving credit to the brand or corporate name for arranging for the performance or event.[49]

As with the other marketing tools, the goal of a sponsorship should be to integrate the cause with the firm's advertising message. It should be easy to recognize the link between the person or group being sponsored, the activity, and the company involved. Also, the marketing team should incorporate all trade and consumer promotions with the event. Sampling is an effective method to use during a sponsorship.

STANDARDIZATION

Standardization is an international expansion strategy. It means a firm creates consistent product and market offerings across countries with the goal of generating economies of scale in production and advertising. An advantage of standardization is that the product will use the same message in all of its markets.

Standardization in advertising means presenting a unified theme across nations and cultures. Although the language may be different, all ads have the same basic theme. Thus an advertisement for a product in France would be the same in Spain, the United States, China, or any other country, except for the language.

The contrast to standardization is adaptation, in which an advertising message is adapted to each individual nation. (*See* ADAPTATION *and* GLOBALLY INTEGRATED MARKETING COMMUNICATIONS *for additional information.*)

STEREOTYPING

One of the criticisms of advertising is that it tends to perpetuate negative stereotypes, especially of women, the elderly, and some minorities. Critics argue that in many advertisements women are portrayed as the weaker gender whose primary responsibility is to care for the children and the home, or as sex objects. The elderly are often depicted as dumb and helpless. Some critics suggest that various ethnic minorities are often portrayed as being inferior to whites.

Although these problems exist to some degree, marketing experts and advertising agencies have made giant strides in recent years to eliminate stereotyping. The question remains as to whether stereotyping still truly exists. Marketers clearly seek to identify specific demographic groups and sell to them. This activity is considered a form of stereotyping by some people. Advertising professionals would counter by stating that advertising to various demographic groups is simply trying to appeal to specific target markets, and if they offend those in the market, their goods or services will not sell. To reach specific market segments effectively requires speaking in the language of the target group, and if it appears to be phony or manipulative it fails.

STIMULUS CODABILITY

One element of a product label is the company's logo. Logos are designed to elicit shared meanings among consumers, which is termed stimulus codability. Logos with high stimulus codability easily evoke consensually held meanings within a culture or subculture (such as the Prudential Rock). A logo should also create positive feelings in the target market.

When a logo has a high degree of codability, it is more easily recognized and can be linked to a particular good or service. A logo with a low degree of codability means the company will spend more money on advertising to create the recognition that comes through familiarity.

STORYBOARD

A storyboard is a series of still photographs or sketches that outline the structure of a television ad. A storyboard illustrates the ad in the early stages of development. It is often used with clients to explain a television ad to gain their approval before actually filming the advertisement. It has become an excellent method of communicating the basic thrust of a television ad.

STRAIGHT REBUY

In a business-to-business purchasing situation, a straight rebuy occurs when a firm has previously chosen a vendor and wishes to reorder. This tends to be a routine process. Only one or two members of the buying center are normally involved in straight rebuys. Often the purchasing agent and the users of the product are the only persons aware of a rebuy order. The user's role is just to inform the buyer of the need to replenish the supply. Contact is then made with the supplier and an order is placed. Evaluation of alternatives or evaluation of information is not pursued. Often orders are placed electronically. (*See* MODIFIED REBUY *and* NEW-TASK PURCHASE *for information about other buying situations.*)

SUBSTANTIATION (OF ADVERTISING CLAIMS)

Every aspect of advertising is regulated by the Federal Trade Commission (FTC). Regardless of the type of communication, unfair or deceptive messages are prohibited. To meet this requirement, advertisers must be able to substantiate claims through competent and reliable evidence. This means that if endorsers are used, their statements must be truthful and represent their experiences or opinions. If expert endorsements are used, those statements must be based on legitimate tests performed by experts in the field. All claims must reflect the typical experience that a customer would expect to encounter from the use of the good or service, unless the advertisement clearly and prominently states otherwise.

One of the keys to FTC evaluations of advertisements and marketing communications is substantiation. Firms must be able to substantiate (e.g., prove or back up) any claims made. Failure to do so can result in some form of FTC action. Various rules can help an agency or firm ensure their advertisements meet the FTC's guidelines on substantiation.

First, the advertiser should be aware of the FTC's substantiation rule. Any factual claims made in an advertisement must be documented through reliable scientific evidence. The substantiation test is especially important in comparative advertising. Any comparisons with a competitor's product must be well documented. Independent third party or neutral sources of information such as *Consumer Reports* will reduce chances of a lawsuit by the competition.

Second, when an advertisement refers to product tests, the person preparing the ad should make sure the tests were unbiased, objective, scientific, statistically sound, and conducted by experts in the field.

Third, be certain any claims that are made would be true for a normal or typical consumer using the product in a normal, typical fashion. If the company claims that using a piece of exercise equipment will create a firmer stomach, they need to be sure those results would occur under normal circumstances for a typical person. Any testimonials or endorsements in an advertisement must meet this typical-person test, or a disclaimer must be provided stating the results were unusual or not ordinary.

Fourth, and finally, price comparisons, do not distort prices. Price comparisons must be made with comparable products and the same size container. Prices should be obtained from the same time period, in approximately the same location, and in the same type of store. Comparing prices to those of companies in other states will probably result in a negative reaction by local competitors and an investigation by the FTC.

SWEEPSTAKES

See CONTESTS AND SWEEPSTAKES.

TAGLINE

The tagline is a phrase in an advertisement that is designed to drive home a key point about the company. It is often short and to the point. It is based on the company's image and the message presented in a specific text. A tagline can be both verbal and written, such as when one appears on the screen accompanied by a voice-over on a television ad. A tagline can be verbal only, on radio or television. Some taglines are found only in print. A brief tagline may appear on a billboard or outdoor advertisement. The tagline for MasterCard is "For everything else, there is MasterCard."

Advertising creatives will spend a considerable amount of time and effort devising a memorable tagline that clearly makes the key point. Effective taglines may carry over from one campaign to the next and may be long recalled by consumers. A stronger brand emerges when a tagline is successful.

TARGET MARKET ANALYSIS

A target market analysis is a component of a marketing plan. This analysis includes examining the various target markets available to a firm. It should involve discovering the needs and wants of various consumer and business groups. A target market analysis defines the benefits that customers are seeking and determines the ways in which they can be reached. The conclusion of the analysis should be an identification of the specific target market the firm will seek to reach. By focusing on these markets, it is possible to accomplish more than if the company tries to serve all possible markets.

From an advertising perspective, once the target market is selected, promotional appeals can be developed that will attract attention and spur sales. The advertisements will be based on an in-depth understanding of the target market. It is important to define the target market in terms of demographics and psychographics. In addition, geographic factors may be important. (*See* MARKET SEGMENTATION *for additional information.*)

TELEVISION ADVERTISING

Television has long been viewed as the most glamorous advertising medium. Television offers advertisers the most extensive coverage and highest reach of any of the media. Millions of viewers can be reached simultaneously with one advertisement. Television provides many opportunities for creativity in advertising design. Visual imugcs and sounds can be incorporated together to gain the attention of viewers as well as to persuade them. Products can be demonstrated on television in a manner that is not possible with print or radio.

Television has many advantages for advertisers. One advantage is intrusion value, which is the ability of a medium or advertisement to intrude upon viewers without their voluntary attention. Television ads with a catchy musical tune, sexy content, or motion also grab the viewer's attention. Another advantage of television advertising is that while ads are more expensive, the cost per contact is relatively low. It is this low cost per contact that justifies spending $2 million for a thirty-second spot on the Super Bowl, which continues to be the most costly television program year after year.

Television also has some disadvantages. For example, clutter remains a major problem, especially on network programs. A commercial break lasting more than five minutes is often packed with eight to fifteen commercials. To make it worse, many viewers switch channels during long commercial breaks. This form of clutter makes it difficult for a single message to have any influence. Also, television commercials have short life spans. Most ads last fifteen or thirty seconds. Occasionally an advertiser will purchase a forty-five- or sixty-second ad, but those are rare.

Another disadvantage of television is the high cost per ad, not only for the media time but also in terms of production costs. Commercials are often expensive to produce. At the same time, since television ads are shown so frequently, they quickly lose the ability to attract the viewer's interest. Consequently, ads must be replaced with something new before consumers get tired of them and tune them out.

When creating television advertisements, advertising agencies attempt to match the client firm's target audience or market segment with specific shows. Each television network and each show tends to attract a specific type of audience. Cable television programming often provides a well-defined, homogeneous audience that matches more narrowly defined target markets.

Television is also used by business-to-business advertisers. They are an effective way to reach members of the business buying center that otherwise cannot be contacted. Since ad clutter in trade journals and traditional business outlets has increased, television spots have become an alternative. Recently, many business advertisers have begun to create emotional appeals in business advertisements.

TESTIMONIAL EXECUTION

A testimonial execution is a type of executional framework. Other types of executional frameworks include animation, slice-of-life, dramatization, authoritative, demonstration, fantasy, and informative. In a testimonial execution, an individual declares that he or she has used a good or service and the result was a positive experience. Testimonials are also used as evidence that the item works, such as when a person states that a particular diet helped him or her lose weight.

Testimonials are often used to promote services. Services are intangible, which means they cannot be seen or touched. Since consumers cannot examine the service before a purchase, testimony from a current customer is an effective method of describing the benefits or attributes of the service. When choosing a dentist, attorney, or automobile repair shop, consumers often ask friends, relatives, or co-workers. A testimonial advertisement simulates a word-of-mouth recommendation.

Testimonials can enhance company credibility. Endorsers and famous individuals do not always have high levels of credibility, because consumers know they are being paid. Instead, a testimonial can be offered by an everyday person who is, or resembles, an actual customer.

The testimonial type of executional framework is also used successfully in the business-to-business sectors. Testimonies from current customers add credibility to the claims being made by the business vendor. In many business buying situations, prospective vendors are asked for references. Testimonials provide references in advance. Since most buyers believe what others say about a company more than they believe what a company says about itself, the testimonial approach often has greater credibility than self-proclamations.

THEATER TEST

Copytesting is a message evaluation methodology that is used when an advertisement is finished or in its final stages of development prior to production. The tests are designed to solicit responses to the main message of the ad as well as the format in which that message is presented.

A theater test is a method of copytesting. The test involves displaying a set of television ads, including the one being evaluated, within some type of television program. Subjects who view the advertisements do not know which one is being evaluated. Theater tests mimic reality in the sense that consumers are normally exposed to multiple messages, such as when a television or radio station plays a series of commercials during a break in programming. The test also allows researchers the opportunity to compare the target piece with other ads. All of the advertisements in the test must be in the same stage of development (e.g., a set of storyboards or a series of nearly completed or completed television ads). Theater tests can be used to see if audiences remember an advertisement. They also can assess whether the subjects had favorable or negative reactions to the ad. (*See* COPY-TESTING *for additional information.*)

THREE-EXPOSURE HYPOTHESIS

The three-exposure hypothesis, as formulated by Herbert Krugman, postulates that it takes a minimum of three exposures for an advertisement to be effective.[50] One exposure is insufficient, because it will not be recalled. Therefore, advertisers often use multiple exposures to ensure consumers and businesses are exposed a sufficient number of times for the ad to become effective. Exactly how many times an advertisement must be seen to be effective is not known. The number varies widely depending on the advertisement itself and the consumer or business that is exposed to the ad. For example, a person who is contemplating the purchase of a new automobile will require fewer exposures to an automobile ad than someone who is not thinking about purchasing a new vehicle.

In many instances, advertisers base placements of ads on the three-exposure hypothesis. For example, if an ad is going to be in only one issue of a magazine, the agency will often purchase three ads within that one issue with the idea that three ads are more likely to be noticed by the reader. Another approach would be to run a single ad in three successive issues.

The three-exposure hypothesis is related to recall, rather than favorable or unfavorable reactions. Advertisers know that commercials with higher intrusion value, humor, and other techniques are more likely to be recalled than other approaches. Still, a minimum of three exposures is their rule of thumb. (*See* INTRUSION VALUE *for additional information.*)

THRESHOLD EFFECT

Threshold effects occur at the level of advertising spending that yields the optimal response from consumers in terms of sales. If too little is spent on advertising the impact on sales will be minimal. If too much is spent, the market becomes saturated with ads and the additional dollars yield less and less impact. This is diminishing returns. The goal of setting an advertising budget is to find the threshold effect, which is the point at which the money spent on advertising yields the maximum results. (*See* CARRYOVER EFFECTS; DECAY EFFECTS; *and* SALES-RESPONSE CURVE *for additional information.*)

TOP CHOICE

When a consumer is asked to specifically name a brand he or she is willing to purchase, the top choice is that brand. A top choice exists within the consumer's evoked set, or the brands that come to mind in a given product category. As an example, an evoked set of automobile manufacturers might include Ford, Chrysler, Toyota, and Honda. A consumer who states he or she always buys Honda cars or is willing to consider Honda is expressing his or her top choice. (*See* EVOKED SET *and* TOP-OF-MIND BRAND *for additional information.*)

TOP-OF-MIND BRAND

The top-of-mind brand is the brand consumers think of first when asked about a particular product category. For example, if asked to identify fast-food restaurants, a subject who replies "McDonald's" is stating his or her top-of-mind brand. The same would be true for a business-to-business buyer who responds that Intel is tops in terms of computer microprocessors.

Several advantages accrue from being top of mind. First, it increases the chances the brand will be purchased. Second, it usually involves a higher level of perceived image, which means in many cases the top-of-mind brands can charge consumers more for their product brand. Third, advertising can focus on reminding consumers about the brand rather than trying to persuade them of the brand's superiority. For instance, Intel can simply use the slogan "Intel inside" and consumers know what it stands for. They no longer have to convince most of us that the Intel product is superior to other brands of microprocessors. (*See* TOP CHOICE *for additional information.*)

TRADE PROMOTION

Trade promotions are the expenditures or incentives used by manufacturers and other members of the marketing channel to help push products through to retailers. Trade promotions entice members of the trade channel to purchase goods for eventual resale. In other words, trade promotions are aimed at retailers, distributors, wholesalers, brokers, or agents. A manufacturer can use trade promotions to convince firms to carry its goods. Wholesalers, distributors, brokers, and agents can use trade promotions to attract retailers to purchase products.

A variety of trade promotional tools exist. These items are used by manufacturers as well as other members of the trade channel. The most common promotional tools are

- trade allowances,
- trade incentives,
- trade contests,
- training programs,
- vendor support programs,
- trade shows,
- specialty advertising, and
- point-of-purchase advertising.

The primary goal of a trade promotion program is to build strong relations with other members of the channel. This includes distributors, wholesalers, brokers, or agents. Promotional programs are designed to entice these middlemen to carry products and push them to retailers.

According to Ernst & Young, between 7 and 10 percent of sales revenues from all branded goods are spent on trade promotions. In other words, for every dollar of sales, seven to ten cents has been spent on trade promotions. Although the exact amount spent on trade promotions is difficult to estimate, it is clear that more money is devoted to trade promotions than any other promotional tool. Many manufacturers have tried to reduce these expenditures. What they find, however, is resistance from retailers, directions from their own sales managers, negative effects on profits, and pressures from their competitors who are still offering trade promotions.[51]

TRADE REGULATION RULING

Trade regulation rulings are a type of action that can be taken by the Federal Trade Commission (FTC) toward an entire industry. Trade regulation rulings are usually the result of an investigation by the FTC of an entire industry or multiple firms within an industry. Rather than deal with each firm individually, it is expedient for the FTC to implicate an entire industry in terms of unfair or deceptive advertising practices.

Normally the FTC holds public hearings and accepts both oral and written arguments from industry lawyers or attorneys from individual firms during an investigation. The commission then makes a ruling that applies to every firm within an industry. As with other rulings by the FTC, decisions can be challenged in the U.S. Court of Appeals.

TRAFFIC MANAGER

A traffic manager works closely with the account executive and other members of an advertising agency. The traffic manager's responsibility is to schedule the various aspects of the agency's work to ensure the work is completed by the target deadline. He or she will provide creatives and other agency employees with information about work to be done and check with them on deadlines. Normally the traffic manager attends meetings with clients along with the account executive to ensure all marketing materials have been prepared in a timely manner and deadlines are being met.

TRANSMISSION DEVICE

In terms of communication, transmission devices are all of the items that carry the message from the sender to the receiver. In a conversation, transmission devices include light waves, sound waves, and ink on a page, along with tastes, smells, and feelings associated with touch.

In advertising, the transmission device is any channel that carries a marketing message. The channel may be a television, a billboard, a Sunday newspaper with a coupon placed in it, a letter to the purchasing agent of a large retail store, or a magazine. To be effective, advertisers must select transmission devices that will be noticed by members of the firm's target market and that will accurately convey the advertising message.

UNAIDED RECALL

One key goal of advertising is to have consumers remember or recall an ad. Several tests are designed to identify how well an ad was remembered. Unaided recall is a methodology in which subjects are asked to name, or recall, the advertisements they saw on television or heard on the radio the previous evening, without being given any prompts or memory jogs.

In print media, there are two approaches to unaided recall tests. In the first, consumers are contacted the day after an ad appeared in a magazine or newspaper. The individuals name the ads they recall and then are asked a series of questions to discover the features of the advertisement they remember. In the second, a subject is provided with a magazine for a certain period of time, normally one week. The individual is instructed to read the magazine as he or she normally would during leisure time. Then the researcher returns and asks a series of questions about which ads were memorable and what features the individual could remember. (*See* AIDED RECALL *for additional information.*)

UNIQUE SELLING PROPOSITION MESSAGE STRATEGY

A message strategy is the primary tactic used in the creation of an advertising message. Message strategies can be divided into four categories: cognitive, affective, conative, and brand. The cognitive message strategies, in turn, can be divided into five subcategories: generic, preemptive, unique selling proposition, hyperbole, and comparative.

The unique selling proposition message strategy is an explicit, testable claim of uniqueness or superiority that can be supported or substantiated in some manner. Brand parity, or the perception that there are no real differences between market offerings, makes a unique selling proposition more difficult to prepare.

In general, a unique selling proposition will include terms such as "exclusive" or "one and only" in the text of the advertisement. To strengthen the claim, the advertiser may suggest that the competition wishes it could copy the product feature, or provides an inferior version.

USE OR APPLICATION POSITIONING STRATEGY

Positioning is the process of creating a perception in the mind of consumers concerning the nature of a brand relative to the competition. Possible positioning approaches include attributes, competitors, use or application, price-quality, product user, product class, and cultural symbol.

Use or application positioning involves the creation of a memorable set of uses for a product. This approach has long been utilized by

Arm & Hammer. The decline in home baking made it necessary to promote sales. Therefore, Arm & Hammer developed new and different uses for baking soda. One of the first was to suggest that it could be used as a deodorizer in the refrigerator, carpet, and even cat litter box.

USER

In the business-to-business buying process, users are the members of the organization who actually use the good or service. When the product is office supplies, users may be the secretarial staff. If the product is the tin used to make tin cans, users are the factory workers in the production facility. Computing staff members run mainframes and computers.

Users often play a central part in the buying process. In straight rebuy situations, users normally inform management or the buyer that it is time to reorder. For modified rebuy situations, users are often involved in the buying process and have a voice in selecting the vendor. For a new buy situation, users are often called on to help develop the specifications for the bidding process.

UTILITY

Utility is the value or expected value associated with the purchase of an item. A product has direct utility when, for example, consuming a soft drink satisfies a person's thirst and creates a sugar buzz. Indirect utility is a secondary outcome, such as when a person thinks that wearing a fashionable and popular brand will cause people to assume that the consumer is well-off financially and has a strong sense of fashion.

Services also offer utility. For instance, an ATM card from a bank has the utility of twenty-four-hour access to cash, plus the ability to conduct other transactions when the bank is closed. People exchange money, in part, for utility in the goods and services they purchase.

VALUES

Values are strongly held beliefs about a topic or concept. Values are linked to the attitudes that lead to judgments and guide personal behaviors. Attitudes are shaped, in part, by an individual's personal values. Values, which are more enduring than attitudes, normally form during childhood. They may change as a person ages and experiences life.

In terms of consumer decision-making processes, both attitudes and values are helpful to advertisers. A product tied to a relatively universal value, such as patriotism, allows the firm to create a linkage between a positive image of the value and that of the product. Since values are strongly held, advertisers must carefully choose which values to emphasize when creating ads. Expressing values is most powerful when the value matches some aspect of the good or service, such as protecting one's family by buying life insurance.

VARIABILITY THEORY

Variability theory suggests that seeing the same advertisement in varied environments increases recall and enhances its effectiveness. This is because the message becomes encoded in the brain through various methods or channels. As a result, it is more likely the message will become part of the consumer's long-term memory.

Creatives utilize variability theory by altering the situational context of a particular ad. For example, an advertising campaign may use various settings to convey the same basic message, such as the recent one prepared by MasterCard: "There are some things money can't buy. For everything else, there's MasterCard." By varying the context of the ad, the goal is to increase consumer recall.[52]

Another application of variability theory is to use additional media. Different media can convey the same message, which is often more effective than repeating an advertisement in the same medium. Multimedia campaigns are also effective in reducing competing ad interference, which occurs when a consumer sees advertisements for more than one brand. Thus, an ad that appears on television and is also in magazines works better than one that appears only on television and has to compete with other brands. (*See* RECENCY THEORY *and* THREE-EXPOSURE HYPOTHESIS *for additional information.*)

VIRAL MARKETING

Viral marketing is an advertisement that is in some way tied to an e-mail. It can be attached to the e-mail or placed in the body of the e-mail. Viral marketing is a form of advocacy or word-of-mouth endorsement marketing. One customer passes along the message to other potential buyers. The name "viral" is derived from the image of a person being infected with the marketing message, then spreading it to friends like a virus. The major difference, however, is that the customer voluntarily sends the message to others. It does not occur automatically.

Viral marketing messages may be hyperlinked promotions that take someone immediately to a Web site, online newsletters, or various games. Statistics indicate that 81 percent of recipients who receive a viral marketing message pass it along to at least one other person. Almost 50 percent pass it along to two or more people. The marketing message can be more deliberate, similar to an individual recommending something to a friend. A viral message can also be transmitted passively by being attached to an e-mail. Viral marketing allows a firm to gain rapid product awareness at a low cost.[53]

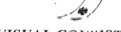

VISUAL CONSISTENCY

Part of the process of evaluating an advertisement is to determine its visual consistency. Visual consistency means that visual images are used consistently from one advertisement to another and from one ad campaign to the next. The visual image may be a logo, a trademark, or even a composite image, such as the hands of Allstate holding a house.

Encountering a specific image or visual display over and over again helps embed it in long-term memory. Visual consistency is important because consumers spend very little time viewing or listening to the message. In most cases, it will be just a casual glance at a print advertisement or at a television ad.

Visual consistency may cause the viewer to move the advertising message from short-term memory to long-term memory. Logos and other longstanding images that appear consistently help fix the brand or company in the consumer's mind.

VISUAL ESPERANTO

Visual Esperanto is a form of universal language. Visual images are more powerful than verbal descriptions. The use of visual Esperanto makes global advertising possible. It is especially important in the international arena, because visual images transcend cultural differences.

To illustrate the power of a visual image compared to a verbal account, think of the word *exotic*. Exotic can mean a white beach in Hawaii. It could also mean a small cabin in the snow-capped mountains of Switzerland. To others, exotic may be a tribal village in Africa. The word can vary in meaning. A picture, on the other hand, of a couple holding hands while walking on a shore has practically the same meaning across all cultures. A young child smiling after eating a piece of candy conveys a relatively universal message.

In advertising, the most important task in creating visual Esperanto is selecting the appropriate image. The creative chooses an image that conveys the intended meaning or message across various cultures. The goal is to create a brand identity through visuals rather than words. Words support the visual image.

The difficult part of visual Esperanto is making sure the image transcends cultures. Once a universal image has been created, the creatives in each country can take the image and modify it to appeal to their target audience.

VISUAL IMAGE

When creating an advertisement, one primary feature is the degree of emphasis given to visual elements as opposed to verbal or written cues. Most major forms of advertising and marketing communications have both visual and verbal elements, with the exception of radio. Verbally oriented ads place greater emphasis on words. The viewer must take time to process the information in an advertisement and focus on the verbal or written elements. An advertisement that is highly visual proceeds differently. Viewers pay more attention to visual cues and less to verbal or written arguments.

Visual images have various advantages for advertisers. For example, they often lead to more favorable attitudes toward both the advertisement and the brand. Furthermore, visuals tend to be more easily remembered than verbal copy. The brain stores visual images as both pictures and words from the ad. This dual processing makes it easier for people to recall the message. Visual images are usually stored in both the left and right sides of the brain, whereas verbal messages tend be stored in only the left side of the brain.

Visual images range from concrete and realistic to abstract. Concrete visuals include persons, places, or things. In an abstract picture or image, the subject is more difficult to recognize. Concrete pictures are more readily recalled than abstract images due to dual-coding processes. Thus, an ad with a picture of spaghetti used in promoting a restaurant will be processed both as a picture and as a verbal representation. Ads with concrete images lead to more favorable attitudes than ads with no pictures or abstract pictures. Thus, research offers many reasons for creatives to include visual images in advertisements.[54]

VULNERABILITY

An advertising appeal based on fear must be sufficiently strong to attract the viewer's attention but not so powerful that the viewer turns away from the advertisement. A model that helps design fear appeals is called the behavioral response model. The goal of this model is to create an advertisement that relies on two elements, vulnerability and severity.

Vulnerability is a calculation made by the viewer, in which he or she considers the odds of being affected by the negative consequences of an action. For example, an advertisement that stresses that drunk driving can lead to a traffic arrest can be designed to make the viewer believe that it would only be a matter of time before he or she will be caught by police when driving impaired. Once a viewer or consumer feels sufficiently vulnerable, fear increases and the individual is more likely to be persuaded by the content of the message. (*See* FEAR APPEAL *for additional information.*)

WARMTH METER

Many times advertisers are interested in eliciting emotional responses to their messages. Physiological arousal tests of advertisements measure the fluctuations in a person's body functions that are associated with changing emotions. A warmth monitor is an alternative method that was developed to measure emotional reactions to advertisements.

The concept behind the warmth meter is that warm, positive feelings may be directed toward an ad or a product. Warmth is measured by subjects manipulating a joystick while watching an advertisement. The movements track reactions to an ad by making marks on a sheet of paper containing four lines. The four lines are labeled

1. absence of warmth,
2. neutral,
3. warmhearted/tender, and
4. emotional.

Although the warmth meter was developed to evaluate television ads, it can be adapted to radio ads.

Individuals are asked to watch a series of advertisements in a theater-type lab featuring a big-screen television. As they watch, if they feel negatively about the ad, they pull the joystick downward. If they feel more positively, the joystick is pushed in the opposite direction. This process allows for a moment-by-moment reaction to an advertisement. The results of the participant's reactions are tallied into one graph and then placed over the advertisement. This technology allows an advertiser to see which parts of the ad elicit positive emotions and which parts elicit negative emotions. Next, the subjects form a focus group to discuss the ad and why they felt the way they did at various moments during the viewing.[55]

An alternative warmth monitor is available over the Internet. As subjects watch the ad on streaming video, a mouse is moved along a tab featuring a sliding scale from one to ten. If viewers like what they see, they slide the scale toward the ten. Those who feel a negative reaction slide the scale toward the one. After the data has been collected, a graph can be superimposed over the advertisement. The results indicate the likable and nonlikable parts of the commercial. Then, if a focus group is needed to discuss the ad, subjects can be selected from the participants. The focus group session can even be held online.[56]

WHEELER-LEA AMENDMENT

The Wheeler-Lea Amendment to Section 5 of the Federal Trade Commission (FTC) Act was passed in 1938. This section prohibits false and misleading advertising. A firm can violate the amendment even if the company did not expressly intend to deceive. An advertisement or communication is deemed to be deceptive or misleading when

1. a substantial number of people or the "typical person" is left with a false impression or misrepresentation about the product.
2. the misrepresentation induces people or the "typical person" to make a purchase.

If one or both conditions are met, the FTC is led to the conclusion that a violation has occurred. To stop a false or misleading ad, an individual or a business can sue to enforce the amendment. In the case of a business-versus-business lawsuit, the competing firm must show either infringement of a trademark or false advertising.

Appendix

Advertising Resources

The following list includes individuals who have recently written articles or textbooks about advertising. This list is not meant to be exhaustive, but is a sampling of individuals who are active in the field of advertising. It was compiled primarily from articles that appeared in the *Journal of Advertising* and the *Journal of Advertising Research* and from membership in the American Academy of Advertising Association.

Abelman, Robert	Cleveland State University
Abernethy, Avery M.	Auburn University
Abratt, Russell	University of the Witwatersrand, Johannesburg, South Africa
Adams, Arthur J.	University of Louisville
Adler, Keith	Michigan State University
Agee, Tom	University of Auckland, New Zealand
Ahuvia, Aaron C.	University of Michigan Business School
Aiken, Damon	Butler University
Aikman-Eckenrode, Shelley N.	University of Texas at El Paso
Alden, Dana L.	University of Hawaii at Manoa
Alexander, Allison	University of Georgia
Allaway, Arthur	University of Alabama
Allen, Charlotte	Stephen F. Austin State University
Allen, Douglas	Bucknell University
Al-Olayan, Fahad S.	King Saud University, Saudi Arabia
Ambler, Tim	London Business School
Anckaert, Pascal	Ghent University
Andrews, J. Craig	Marquette University
Angur, Madhukar G.	University of Michigan–Flint
Anschuetz, Ned	DDB Needham, Chicago
Appiah, Osei	Iowa State University
Arbittier, Jerry	Competitive Media Reporting
Arias-Bolzmann, Leopoldo	Universidad Adolfo Ibanez, Chile

Ashley, Susan R.	rsc The Quality Measurement Company, Europe
Assael, Henry	New York University
Atkin, David J.	Cleveland State University
Austin, Erica Weintraub	Washington State University
Avery, Jim	University of Oklahoma
Aylesworth, Andrew B.	Bentley College
Baack, Donald	Pittsburg State University
Babin, Laurie A.	University of Southern Mississippi
Backhaus, Klaus	University of Muenster, Germany
Badzinski, Diane M.	Westfield State College
Bailey, Scott	Targetbase Marketing
Baker, Michael J.	Nottingham Business School
Baker, William E.	University of Vermont
Bakker, Arnold B.	Utrecht University, Netherlands
Balasubramanian, Siva K.	Southern Illinois University
Baldinger, Allan L.	The NPD Group
Baltas, George	Athens University of Economics and Business, Athens, Greece
Bao, Yeoing	University of Alabama–Huntsville
Barnard, Neil	Consultant
Barone, Michael J.	Iowa State University
Barry, Thomas E.	Southern Methodist University
Bates, Nancy	U.S. Census Bureau
Bathe, Stefan	Roper Starch Worldwide
Bauerly, Ronald J.	Western Illinois University
Beard, Fred K.	University of Oklahoma
Bearden, William O.	University of South Carolina
Becker, Boris W.	Oregon State University
Bellizzi, Joseph A.	Arizona State University–West
Beltramini, Richard F.	Wayne State University
Benjamin, Louise M.	University of Georgia
Bennett, Richard	Market Facts of Canada Ltd.
Bergin, Kevin	Pitcher and Crow, New York
Berkowitz, David	University of Alabama–Huntsville
Berry, Lissete	Lissete Berry and Associates, Inc.
Berthon, Pierre	Columbia Business School
Besser, Donna	Smithsonian Institution
Bevans, Michael	San Francisco State University
Bezjian-Avery, Alexa	DePaul University
Bhargava, Mukesh	Oakland University, Rochester, Michigan
Bhat, Subodh	San Francisco State University

Bhatnagar, Amit	University of Wisconsin–Milwaukee
Biehal, Gabriel J.	University of Maryland at College Park
Biocca, Frank	Michigan State University
Biswas, Abhijit	Lousiana State University
Blair, Edward	University of Houston
Blair, Margaret Henderson	rsc The Quality Measurement Company
Blenkhorn, David L.	Wilfrid Laurier University, Canada
Bloom, Helen	Consultant
Bogart, Leo	Author
Boivin, Yvan	University of Sherbrooke, Canada
Bone, Paula Fitzgerald	West Virginia University
Bower, Amanda M.	Lousiana State University
Brackett, Lana K.	Roger Williams University
Bridges, Sheri	Wake Forest University
Briggs, Rex	Millward Brown
Bristol, Terry	University of Arkansas at Little Rock
Broadbent, Simon	Leo Burnett, London, BrandCon Limited
Bronn, Peggy Simcic	Norwegian School of Management
Brotherton, Timothy P.	University of Alabama
Brouwer, Marten	University of Amsterdam
Brown, Stephen	University of Ulster, Northern Ireland
Browne, Beverly A.	Oregon State University
Brumbaugh, Anne M.	Case Western Reserve University
Brunel, Frederic F.	Boston University School of Management
Bruner, Gordon C., II	Southern Illinois University at Carbondale
Bruzzone, Donald E.	Bruzzone Research Company
Buckley, Sara K.	U.S. Treasury Department
Buda, Richard	Hofstra University
Bunett, John	University of Denver
Burke, Jeffrey	Saint Joseph's University
Burne, Tom	The Open University
Burns, Alvin C.	Louisiana State University
Burton, Scot	University of Arkansas
Bush, Alan J.	University of Memphis
Bush, Victoria D	University of Mississippi
Busler, Michael	Cabrini College
Calder, Bobby	Northwestern University
Cannon, Hugh M.	Wayne State University
Carlson, Jay P.	Bradley University

Carlson, Les	Clemson University
Carr, Benjamin, Jr.	Roger Williams University
Cary, Mark S.	Chavda and Cary Research and Consulting
Casey, Susan L.	Old Dominion University
Chakraborty, Goutam	Oklahoma State University
Chao, Paul	University of Northern Iowa
Chapman, Patricia S.	Mantz Research
Chaudhuri, Ariun	Fairfield University
Chen, Qimei	University of Minnesota
Cho, Bongjin	Keimyung University
Cho, Chang-Hoan	University of Florida
Cicic, Muris	University of Wollongong, Australia
Clark, John M.	University of Missouri–Kansas City
Clow, Kenneth E.	University of Louisiana at Monroe
Coderre, Francois	University of Sherbrooke, Canada
Coffey, Steve	PC Meter
Collins, James M.	University of Alaska–Fairbanks
Colombo, Richard	Fordham University
Cook, William A.	Advertising Research Foundation
Cornelissen, Joep P.	Manchester Metropolitan University, United Kingdom
Cornwell, T. Bettina	University of Memphis, University of Queensland
Coulter, Keith S.	Clark University
Coulter, Robin A.	University of Connecticut
Cowan, Deanna	University of the Witwatersrand, Johannesburg, South Africa
Coyle, James R.	Baruch College, City University of New York
Crites, Stephen L., Jr.	University of Texas at El Paso
Crutchfield, Tammy Neal	Mercer University
Curran, Catharine M.	Creigton University
Dacin, Peter	Texas A&M
Dahlen, Micael	Stockholm School of Economics
D'Amico, Theodore F.	Mediamark Research, Inc.
Danaher, Peter J.	University of Auckland
Daubek, Hugh G.	Purdue University
Daugherty, Terry	Vanderbilt University
Davies, Mark	Loughborough University Business School, United Kingdom
Davis, John	Lazarus Marketing Group
Day, Ellen	University of Georgia

De Pelsmacker, Patrick — University of Antwerp and Ghent University

Dean, Dwane Hal — Louisiana State University

Deckinger, E. L. — St. Johns University

DeLorme, Denise E. — University of Central Florida

Derbaix, Christian — Catholic University of Mons, Belgium

Dick, Steven J. — Southern Illinois University at Carbondale

Donius, James F. — Marketplace Measurement Worldwide

Donnelly, William J. — Temple University

Donthu, Naveen — Georgia State University

Dou, Wenyu — University of Wisconsin–Milwaukee; St. Cloud State University; University of Nevada–Las Vegas

Doyle, Kenneth O. — University of Minnesota–Twin Cities

Dreze, Xavier — University of Southern California

D'Souza, Giles — University of Alabama

du Plessis, Erik — Impact Information, South Africa

Duke, Lisa — University of Florida

Duncan, Thomas R. — University of Colorado

Dutka, Solomon — Audits and Surveys Worldwide

Dyson, Paul — Millward Brown International

Eastman, Jacqueline K. — Valdosta State University

Eaton, John — Arizona State University

Echambadi, Raj — University of Central Florida

Edwards, Steven M. — Michigan State University

Ehrenberg, Andrew — South Bank University, London

Eighmey, John — Iowa State University

Elcombe, Ron — Winona State University

Ellen, Pam Scholder — Georgia State University

Elliott, Michael T. — University of Missouri–St. Louis

Englis, Basil G. — Berry College

English, Elaine P. — Law Offices of Elaine P. English

Ephron, Erwin — Ephron, Papazian, and Ephron

Erdogan, B. Zafer — Dumlupinar University of Turkey

Ertel, Chris — Global Business Network

Eves, Anmarie — California State University–Sacramento

Ewing, Michael — Curtin University of Technology, Perth, Australia

Faber, Ronald J. — University of Minnesota

Fam, Kim Shyan — University of Otago, Dunedin, New Zealand

Fan, David P. — University of Minnesota

Farr, Andy — Millward Brown International
Fennis, Bob M. — Free University, Amsterdam
Ferley, Stephen — PMB Print Measurement Bureau
Fernandez, Karen V. — University of Waikato, New Zealand
Fischer, Paul M. — CEO, Center for Primary Care, Evans, Georgia

Fletcher, James E. — University of Georgia
Ford, John B. — Old Dominion University
Foster, Charles — Impact Information
Foster, Dale — Memorial University of Newfoundland
Fox, Richard J. — University of Georgia
Franke, George R. — University of Alabama, Tuscaloosa
Frankel, Lester — Audits and Surveys Worldwide
Frazer, Charles F. — University of Oregon
Friedman, Larry — Ross Cooper Lund
Frisby, Cynthia — Missouri School of Journalism
Fullerton, Ronald A. — University of the South Pacific, Suva, Fiji Islands

Gallagher, Katherine K. — Memorial University of Newfoundland
Garcia, Adriana — United Parcel Service
Gardener, Elizabeth — State University of New York at Buffalo

Garretson, Judith Anne — Louisiana State University
Geason, James A. — University of Florida
Gelb, Betsy — University of Houston
Gentry, James W. — University of Nebraska–Lincoln
Gerritsen, Marinel — University of Nijmagen, Netherlands
Geuens, Maggie — Ghent University
Ghose, Sanjoy — University of Wisconsin–Milwaukee
Gijsbers, Inge — University of Nijmagen, Netherlands
Gilliland, David I. — Colorado State University
Gilmore, Jennifer Marie — University of Illinois at Urbana–Champaign

Goldsmith, Ronald E. — Florida State University
Goodstein, Ronald C. — Georgetown University
Gould, Stephen J. — Baruch College, City University of New York

Grabner-Krauter, Sonja — University of Klagenfurt, Austria
Gray, Stuart — BBDO
Green, Corliss L. — Georgia State University
Grein, Andrew F. — Baruch College, City University of New York

Grier, Sonya A. — Stanford University

Griffin, Tom	Pace University
Grossman, Randi Priluck	Seton Hall University
Grove, Stephen J.	Clemson University
Gugel, Craig	Bates USA
Gulas, Charles S.	Wright State University
Gupta, Pola B.	University of Northern Iowa
Gupta, Reetika	Baruch College, City University of New York
Gwinner, Kevin P.	Kansas State University
Ha, Louisa	University of Oklahoma–Norman
Haefner, James	University of Illinois at Urbana–Champaign
Haley, Eric	University of Tennesee at Knoxville
Hall, Bruce	Howard, Merrell, and Partners
Hamilton, Kate	Ignite
Hardesty, David M.	University of Miami
Harris, Philip G.	Swinburne University of Technology
Harris, Sharon	University of Memphis
Harvey, Bill	Next Century Media
Hazlett, Richard L.	Johns Hopkins University School of Medicine and Hazlett Research Technologies
Hazlett, Sasha Yassky	Hazlett Research Technologies
Heckler, Susan	Georgetown University
Helmig, Bernd	Albert Ludwigs University, Freiburg, Germany
Henthorne, Tony L.	University of Southern Mississippi
Hetsroni, Amir	Yezreel Valley College, Israel
Hildago, Pedro	University of Chile
Hirschman, Elizabeth C.	Rutgers University
Hocutt, Mary Ann	Samford University
Hoerrner, Keisha	Louisiana State University
Hoffer, George E.	Virginia Commonwealth University
Holbrook, Morris B.	Columbia University
Holland, Jonna	University of Nebraska–Omaha
Hollis, Nigel	Millward Brown International
Honeycutt, Earl D., Jr.	Old Dominion University
Hong, Jongpil	University of Texas at Austin
Hoy, Marlea Grubbs	University of Tennesee at Knoxville
Hoyer, Wayne D.	University of Texas at Austin
Huang, Xueli	Edith Cowan University
Huey, Bill	Knapp, Inc.
Huff, Leonard C.	University of Hawaii at Manoa

Huhmann, Bruce A.	University of Alabama
Hung, Kineta	University of Hong Kong
Hwang, Jang-Sun	University of Tennessee
Iacobucci, Dawn	Northwestern University
Ilfeld, Johanna S.	University of California at Berkeley
Jackson, Sally	University of Arizona
James, William L.	Hofstra University
Jancic, Zlatko	University of Ljubljana, Slovenia
Jasperson, Amy E.	University of Texas–San Antonio
Ji, Mindy F.	Texas A&M
Jin, Guang Xi	Institute of Research Continuing Education, Shanghai, China
Johar, Gita Venkataramani	Columbia University Graduate School of Business
Johnson, Madeline	University of Houston–Downtown
Jones, John Philip	Syracuse University
Jones, Marilyn Y.	Bond University School of Business, Queensland, Australia
Jun, Sunkyo	Hannam University
Kahle, Lynn R.	University of Oregon
Kaid, Lynda Lee	University of Florida
Kalra, Ajay	Carnegie Mellon University
Kang, Jikyeong	University of Manchester, United Kingdom
Kanso, Ali	University of Texas at San Antonio
Karande, Kiran	Old Dominion University
Karson, Eric J.	Florida Atlantic University
Kates, Steven M.	Griffith University, Queensland, Australia
Keller, Kevin Lane	Amos Tuck School, Dartmouth College
Kelley, Scott W.	University of Kentucky
Kempf, DeAnna S.	Iowa State University
Kennedy, Rachel	University of South Australia
Kent, Robert J.	University of Delaware
Kibarian, Thomas M.	Management Consultant
Kidd, Pat	Wirthlin Worldwide
Kim, Bong-Hyun	Diamond Advertising Agency, Seoul, South Korea
Kim, Choong-Ryun	Woosuk University, Chonbuk, Korea
Kim, Dongwook	Michigan Technological University
Kim, Joo Young	University of Florida
Kim, Joo-Ho	SK Corporation
Kim, Koanghyub	University of Oklahoma

Kim, Youn-Kyung	University of North Texas
King, Karen Whitehill	University of Georgia
Kirmani, Amna	Southern Methodist University
Kitchen, Philip	Strathclyde University, United Kingdom
Kohli, Chiranjeev	California State University–Fullerton
Kolbe, Richard H.	Kent State University
Kolessar, Ronald S.	The Arbitron Company
Kolligan, Mark	CVS Inc.
Korgaonkar, Pradeep K.	Florida Atlantic University
Korzilius, Hubert	University of Nijmagen, Netherlands
Kosenko, Rustan	Bradley University
Kover, Arthur J.	Fordham University
Kranenburg, Kris	Southern Illinois University at Carbondale
Krishnan, H. Shanker	Indiana University
Kropp, Fredric	Monterrey Institute of International Studies
Krugman, Dean M.	University of Georgia
Kumar, Anand	Southern Illinois University at Carbondale
Kusumoto, Kazuya	Dentsu, Inc.
Kwak, Kyokjin	Drexel University
Kwiatkowski, Kevin	Warner-Lambert
Kwon, Up	Keimyung University
La Ferle, Carrie	Michigan State University
La Tour, Michael S.	Auburn University
LaBahn, Douglas	California State University–Fullerton
Laband, David N.	Auburn University
Labarbera, Prischilla A.	New York University
Laczniak, Russell N.	Iowa State University
Lafferty, Barbara A.	University of South Florida
Laforet, Silvie	Birmingham University, England
Lai, Mengkuan	National Cheng Kung University
Landreth, Stacy	Lousiana State University
Langer, Judith	Langer Associates, Inc.
Lardinoit, Thierry	ESSEC, France
Lariscy, Ruth Ann Weaver	University of Georgia
Lavidge, Robert J.	Elrick and Lavidge
Lavoie, Sylvie	Riviere du Loupe College
Lawrie, Jennifer M.	University of Auckland
Lea, Tony	Compusearch Micromarketing, Data and Systems
Leckenby, John D.	University of Texas at Austin

Lee, Dong-Jin	University of Western Australia
Lee, Joo-Hyun	Michigan State University
Lee, Jung-Gyo	University of Missouri
Lee, Ruby P. W.	Washington State University
Lee, Wei-Na	University of Texas at Austin
Lee, Yih Hwai	National University of Singapore
Leigh, Thomas W.	University of Georgia
Leong, Elaine K. F.	Edith Cowan University
Lerman, Dawn	Baruch College, City University of New York
Lessig, V. Parker	University of Kansas
Lewis, Loran E.	Southern Illinois University at Carbondale
Li, Hairong	Michigan State University
Lichtenstein, Donald R.	University of Colorado
Lin, Carolyn A.	Cleveland State University
Linn, Randy	Wells Fargo Bank
Litman, Barry R.	Michigan State University, East Lansing
Lock, Andrew R.	Manchester Metropolitan University, United Kingdom
Locznaik, Russell	Iowa State University
Lodish, Leonard M.	The Wharton School, University of Pennsylvania
Lohse, Gerald L.	The Wharton School, University of Pennsylvania
Longman, Kenneth A.	Longman-Moran Analytics, Inc.
Loraas, Tina	Auburn University
Low, George S.	Texas Christian University
Lowrey, Pamela	University of Illinois at Urbana–Champaign
Lowrey, Tina M.	Rider University
Lindquist, Jay D.	Western Michigan University
Luna, David	University of Wisconsin–Milwaukee
Luo, Xueming	State University of New York, Fredonia
Lutz, Richard J.	University of Florida
Lynch, Kate	Leo Burnett Media, Chicago
Lynch, Patrick D.	Accenture Institute for Strategic Change
MacKenzie, Scott B.	Indiana University
Maclaran, Pauline	DeMontfort University, Leicester, United Kingdom
Madden, Charles S.	Baylor University

Maddox, Lynda M.	George Washington University
Madrigal, Robert	University of Oregon
Maignan, Isabelle	Florida State University
Mangleburg, Tamara F.	Florida Atlantic University
Manning, Kenneth C.	Colorado State University
Marchand, June	Université Laval
Maroney, Denman	D'Arcy Masius Benton and Bowles
Marshall, Roger	Nanyang Technological University, Singapore
Martin, Brett A. S.	University of Auckland, New Zealand
Martin, Craig	University of Memphis
Martin, Mary C.	University of North Carolina at Charlotte
Maso-Fleischman, Roberta	Qualitative Research Consultant
Mathews, Ryan	First Matter LLC
Mathur, Ike	Southern Illinois University at Carbondale
Mathur, Lynette Knowles	Southern Illinois University at Carbondale
Maynard, Michael L.	Temple University
McArthur, David N.	University of South Carolina
McDonald, Colin	McDonald Research
McDonald, Scott	Time Warner, Inc.
McDowell, Walter S.	University of Miami
McKeage, Kim	University of Maine
McManamon, Mary K.	Lake Erie College
McMillan, Sally J.	University of Tennessee
McNeal, James U.	Texas A&M
McQuarrie, Edward F.	Santa Clara University
Meadow, H. Lee	Eastern Illinois University
Mehta, Abhilasha	Gallup and Robinson, Inc.
Mehta, Darshan	Marketal
Meirick, Patrick	University of Minnesota
Menon, Satya	University of Illinois–Chicago
Miller, Stephen	Lieberman Research, Inc.
Milner, Laura M.	University of Alaska–Fairbanks
Miniard, Paul W.	Florida International University
Miracle, Gordon E.	Michigan State University
Mitchell, Nancy	University of Nebraska–Lincoln
Miyazaki, Anthony D.	University of Miami
Mizuno, Yutaka	Kyoto Institute of Technology
Mohr, Jakki J.	University of Montana
Moon, Young Sook	Hanyang University, Korea

Morgan, Angela G.	Clemson University
Morgan, Fred W.	Michigan State University
Morgan, Robert M.	University of Alabama
Morgan, Susan E.	University of Kentucky
Moriarty, Sandra E.	University of Colorado
Morris, Jon D.	University of Florida
Morrison, Margaret	University of Tennessee at Knoxville
Mowen, John C.	Oklahoma State University
Muehling, Darrel D.	Washington State University
Muhfeld, Katrin	University of Muenster, Germany
Mukherjee, Ashesh	McGill University
Munch, James M.	University of Texas at Arlington
Muncy, James A.	Valdosta State University
Na, Woonburg	Silla University, Korea
Naccarato, John L.	Liggett Stashower, Inc.
Naples, Michael J.	Naples Consulting
Napoli, Julie	Curtin University of Technology, Perth, Australia
Napoli, Philip M.	Fordham University
Nataraajan, Rajan	Auburn University
Neal, William D.	SDR, Inc.
Needel, Stephen P.	Simulation Research, Inc.
Neijens, Peter C.	University of Amsterdam
Nelson, Michelle R.	University of Wisconsin–Madison
Nelson, Richard A.	Louisiana State University
Netemeyer, Richard G.	Louisiana State University
Neuendorf, Kimberly A.	Cleveland State University
Newell, Stephen J.	Bowling Green State University
Nielson, Ulrik Ollie	ALTO CSI, Inc.
Oakenfull, Gillian	Miami University
O'Cass, Aron	Griffith University
O'Guinn, Thomas C.	University of Illinois
Olson, Erik L.	Norwegian School of Management
O'Neill, Harry	Roper ASW
Onkvisit, Sak	San Jose State University
Otnes, Cele C.	University of Illinois at Urbana–Champaign
Padgett, Dan	Tulane University
Papatla, Purushottam	University of Wisconsin–Milwaukee
Parente, Donald E.	Middle Tennessee State
Park, Sea Bum	University of Illinois at Urbana–Champaign
Parker, Betty J.	Western Michigan University

Parsons, Amy L.	Kings College
Parsons, Jeffrey	Memorial University of Newfoundland
Pasadeos, Yorgo	University of Alabama
Patchen, Robert H.	The Arbitron Company
Pawlowski, Donna R.	Creighton University
Pecheux, Claude	Catholic University of Mons, Belgium
Peltier, James	University of Wisconsin–Whitewater
Peracchio, Laura A.	University of Wisconsin–Milwaukee
Phelps, Joe	University of Alabama
Phillips, Barbara J.	University of Saskachewan
Philport, Joseph C.	Competitive Media Reporting
Pickett, Gregory M.	Clemson University
Pinkleton, Bruce	Washington State University
Pisani, Joseph R.	University of Florida
Pokrywczynski, James	Marquette University
Poltrack, David F.	CBS
Pratt, Michael D.	Virginia Commonwealth University
Prendergast, Gerard	Hong Kong Baptist University
Preston, Christopher	Queen Margaret University College, Edinburgh, Scotland
Prince, Mel	Connecticut State University
Prosser, Elise	University of San Diego
Pruitt, Stephen W.	University of Missouri–Kansas City
Quester, Pascale G.	University of Adelaide
Rabuck, Michael J.	The Quality Measurement Company
Rahtz, Don	College of William and Mary
Rangan, Nanda	Ohio University
Raymond, Mary Anne	Clemson University
Reichel, Walter	The A-to-S UNK, Inc.
Reichert, Tom	University of North Texas
Reid, Leonard N.	University of Georgia
Rice, Butch	Research Surveys Ltd.
Richards, Jef I.	University of Texas at Austin
Richardson, Bruce C.	Information Resources, Inc.
Riedesel, Paul	Action Marketing Research, Inc.
Rodgers, Shelley	University of Minnesota, Twin Cities
Roe, Darrell	Marist College
Roehm, Michelle L.	Wake Forest University
Rose, Gregory M.	University of Mississippi
Rose, Randall L.	University of South Carolina
Rosen, Dennis L.	University of Kansas
Rosenburg, Karl E.	The Quality Measurement Company
Rosenfeld, Irene B.	Kraft Canada

Rossiter, John R.	University of Wollongong
Rotfeld, Herbert J.	Auburn University
Roy, Donald P.	Middle Tennessee State University
Rubinson, Joel	The NPD Group
Sadler, Archie	West Virginia University
Sankaralingam, Avu	Charles Schwab and Company
Saunders, John	Aston University, Birmingham, England
Schibrowsky, Don E.	University of Nevada–Las Vegas
Schindler, Robert M.	Rutgers University–Camden
Schroeder, Gary	Information Resources, Inc.
Schultz, Don	Northwestern University
Scipione, Paul	Monclair State University
Scott, Douglas R.	Millward Brown
Scott, Linda	University of Illinois at Urbana–Champaign
Scriven, John	South Bank University, London
Sen, Kapir C.	Lamar University
Sengupta, Sanjit	San Francisco State University
Shamdasani, Prem N.	National University of Singapore
Shao, Alan T.	University of North Carolina at Charlotte
Shapiro, Stewart	University of Delaware
Shaver, Mary Alice	Michigan State University
Shavitt, Sharon	University of Illinois at Urbana–Champaign
Shaw, John J.	Providence College
Shaw-Garlock, Glenda	University of Northern British Columbia, Canada
Sheehan, Kim Bartel	University of Oregon
Sheinin, Daniel A.	University of Maryland at College Park
Sheldon, Kennon	University of Missouri, Columbia
Shen, Fuyhan	Pennsylvania State University
Shi, Yizheng	Hong Kong Baptist University
Shimp, Terence A.	University of South Carolina
Sidler, John	Southern Illinois University at Carbondale
Silberstein, Richard B.	Swinburne University of Technology
Singh, Mandeep	Western Illinois University
Singh, Surendra N.	University of Kansas
Sirgy, M. Joseph	Virginia Polytechnic Institute and State University
Smit, Edith G.	University of Amsterdam

Smith, Bruce L.	Southwest Texas State University
Smith, Rachel	University of Memphis
Sneed, Paula	Kraft Foods
Solomon, Debbie	J. Walter Thompson
Solomon, Michael R.	Auburn University
Soman, Dilip	Hong Kong University of Science and Technology
Son, Youngseok	Dongeui University, Korea
Sonner, Brenda S.	Troy State University
Sood, Sanjay	Rice University
Sorescu, Alina B.	University of Houston
Spake, Deborah F.	Western Michigan University
Spears, Nancy	University of North Texas
Speck, Paul Surgi	University of Missouri–St. Louis
Spilger, Ursula	University of Houston–Downtown
Spittler, Jayne Z.	Leo Burnett Media, Chicago
Spotts, Harlan E.	University of Wisconsin–Parkside
Srinivasan, Srini S.	Drexel University
Stafford, Marla Royne	University of Memphis
Stafford, Thomas F.	University of Memphis
Stanaland, Andrea J.S.	University of Houston
Stanners, Paul-John	Webmate
Stanton, John L.	Saint Joseph's University
Stapel, Jan	Netherlands Institute of Public Opinion
Steinard, Edward A.	National Account Manager, Kellogg Company
Stern, Barbara B.	Rutgers, The State University of New Jersey
Stern, Bruce	Portland State University
Stevens, Lorna	University of Ulster, Northern Ireland
Stevenson, Julie S.	Muskingum Area Technical College
Stevenson, Thomas H.	University of North Carolina at Charlotte
Stewart, David W.	University of Southern California
Stipp, Horst	NBC
Stole, Inger L.	University of Illinois at Urbana–Champaign
Stoltman, Jeffrey J.	Syracuse University
Stone, Gerald	Southern Illinois University at Carbondale
Sukhdial, Ajay	Oklahoma State University
Sumner, David E.	Ball State University
Sun, Tao	University of Minnesota

Sutherland, Max	Monash and Swinburne Universities, Australia
Swayne, Linda E.	University of North Carolina at Charlotte
Tagg, Stephen	University of Strathclyde
Tallyn, Deborah J.	Pacific Bell Directory
Tan, Chee-Ming	ALTO CSI, Inc.
Tan, Juliana	National University of Singapore
Taylor, Charles R.	Villanova University
Taylor, Ronald E.	University of Tennessee at Knoxville
Tedesco, John C.	Virginia Tech.
Tellis, Gerard	University of Southern California
Tharpe, Marye	University of Texas at Austin
Thjomoe, Hans Mathias	Norwegian School of Management
Thompson, Beverly	University of Western Sydney, Nepean
Thompson, Craig J.	University of Wisconsin–Madison
Thorson, Esther	University of Missouri
Till, Brian D.	Saint Louis University
Tinkham, Spencer F.	University of Georgia
Tom, Gail	California State University at Sacramento
Toncar, Mark F.	Lycoming College
Torres, Ivonne M.	University of Houston
Treise, Debbie	University of Florida
Tripp, Carolyn	Western Illinois University
Trivedi, Minakshi	State University of New York at Buffalo
Tscheulin, Dieter K.	Albert Ludwigs University, Freiburg, Germany
Tse, Alan Ching Biu	Chinese University of Hong Kong, Shatin, Hong Kong
Tuckel, Peter	Hunter College, City University of New York
Turley, L. W.	Western Kentucky University
Um, Nam-Hyun	Cheil Communications, Seoul
Urban, David J.	Virginia Commonwealth University
Van Auken, Stuart	California State University at Chico
van Doorn, Jenny	University of Muenster, Germany
van Meurs, Frank	University of Nijmagen, Netherlands
van Meurs, Lex	Infomart, Netherlands
Van Ness, Robert	Kansas State University
Vanden Bergh, Bruce G.	Michigan State University
Vertinsky, Ilan	University of British Columbia

Voli, Patricia Kramer	Old Dominion University
von Gonten, Michael F.	Michael von Gonten, Inc.
Waller, David S.	University of Newcastle, Durimbah, Australia
Walsh, Ann D.	Western Illinois University
Wansink, Brian	University of Illinois at Urbana–Champaign
Warden, Clyde A.	Chaoyang University of Technology
Wardlow, Daniel D.	San Francisco State University
Watson, Barry	Environics Research Group
Watt, Marilyn	Epsilon Group, Inc.
Weilbacher, William M.	Bismark Corporation
Weinberger, Marc G.	University of Massachusetts–Amherst
Weingard, Peter	DDB Needham Worldwide
Wells, William B.	University of Minnesota
Wells, William D.	University of Minnesota
West, Douglas	University of Westminster Business School, London
Whipple, Thomas W.	Cleveland State University
White, Alisa	University of Texas at Arlington
Wicks, Jan LeBlanc	University of Arkansas
Widgery, Robin	Marketing Resources Corporation
Wilson, Elizabeth J.	Boston College
Wilson, R. Dale	Michigan State University
Winer, Russell S.	University of California at Berkeley
Wolburg, Joyce M.	Marquette University
Wolin, Lori	Florida Atlantic University
Woo, Chongmoo	University of Florida
Wood, Leslie	The A-to-S UNK, Inc.
Woodside, Arch G.	Boston College
Wright, Gary	Procter & Gamble
Wright, Newell	James Madison University
Wu, Wann-Yih	National Cheng Kung University
Yamaki, Toshio	Tokyo Kezai University
Yang, Sixian	St. Cloud State University
Yarsuvat, Duygun	University of Istanbul, Turkey
Yin, Jiafei	Central Michigan University
Yoon, Sung-Joon	Kyonggi University
Yorkston, Eric A.	New York University
Youn, Seounmi	University of North Dakota
Young, Charles E.	Ameritrest
Zabkar, Vesna	University of Ljubljana, Slovenia
Zaltman, Gerald	Harvard Business

Zhang, Weijiong	China Europe International Business School
Zhang, Yong	Hofstra University
Zhao, Xinshu	University of Minnesota, University of North Carolina
Zhou, Donsheng	City University of Hong Kong
Zinkhan, George M.	University of Georgia

Notes

1. Mercie Brucks, "The Effect of Product Class Knowledge on Information Search Behavior," *Journal of Consumer Research,* 12 (June 1985), 1-15.

2. Eugene F. Brigham and James L. Pappas, *Managerial Economics,* Second Edition (Hinsdale, IL: Dryden Press, 1976).

3. Al Rics, "Should Your Ads Be an Inside Job?" *Sales and Marketing Management,* 147 (July 10, 1999), 26-27.

4. Ronald L. Zallocco, "Benefit Segmentation of the Fitness Market," *Journal of Health Care Marketing,* 12 (December 1992), 80.

5. David Martin, "Branding: Finding That One Thing," *Brandweek,* (February 16, 1998), 18.

6. Dhruv Grewal and Sukumar Kavanoor, "Comparative versus Noncomparative Advertising: A Meta-Analysis," *Journal of Marketing,* 61 (October 1997), 1-15; Mark Dolliver, "So, If You Can't Say Something Nice . . ." *Adweek—Eastern Edition,* 39 (April 6, 1998), 21.

7. Roger A. Slavens, "Getting a Grip on Co-op," *Modern Tire Dealer,* 75 (March 1994), 34-37.

8. Kapil Bawa and Srini S. Srinivasan, "Coupon Attractiveness and Coupon Proneness: A Framework for Modeling Coupon Redemption," *Journal of Marketing Research,* 34 (November 1997), 517-525; "Coupon Use Seen Growing," *Editor & Publisher,* 129 (November 23, 1996), 16-17; "DSN Charts: Coupons," *Discount Store News,* 38 (May 3, 1999), 4.

9. Steven P. Brown and Douglas M. Stayman, "Antecedents and Consequences of Attitude Toward the Ad: A Meta Analysis," *Journal of Consumer Research,* 19 (June 1992), 34-51.

10. The PACT Agencies, "PACT: Positioning Advertisting Copy Testing," *Journal of Marketing,* 11 (1982), 4-29.

11. Kate Fitzgerald and Nick Lico, "The Big Event," *Automotive News,* 73 (March 29, 1999), AM24-AM25.

12. Kim Pryor, "Events as Incentives," *Incentive,* 173 (August 1999), 102-103.

13. J. Levine, "Fantasy, Not Flesh," *Forbes,* 145 (January 22, 1990), 3-5.

14. Jerry Olson and Thomas J. Reynolds, "Understanding Consumers' Cognitive Structures: Implications for Advertising Strategy," in *Advertising Consumer Psychology,* L. Percy and A. Woodside, Eds. (Lexington, MA: Lexington Books, 1983), pp. 77-90; Thomas J. Reynolds and Alyce Craddock, "The Application of the MECCAS Model to Development and Assessment of Advertising Strategy," *Journal of Advertising Research,* 28 (1988), 43-54.

15. Michael S. Latour and Robin L. Snipes, "Don't Be Afraid to Use Fear Appeals: An Experimental Study," *Journal of Advertising Research,* 36 (March/April 1996), 59-68.

16. Corliss L. Green, "Media Exposure's Impact on Perceived Availability and Redemption of Coupons by Ethnic Consumers," *Journal of Advertising Research,* 35 (March/April 1995), 56-64.

17. Laura Koss-Feder, "Want to Catch Gen X? Try Looking on the Web," *Marketing News,* 32 (December 1992), 80.

18. Bradley Johnson, "IBM Moves Back to Intel Co-op Deal," *Advertising Age,* 68 (March 10, 1997), 4.

19. Tibbett L. Speer, "Growing the Green Market," *American Demographic,* (August 1997) (www.demographics.com).

20. Harlan E. Spotts and Marc G. Weinberger, "Assessing the Use and Impact of Humor on Advertising Effectiveness," *Journal of Advertising,* 26 (Fall 1997), 17-32.

21. Hillary Chura and Mercedes M. Cardona, "Online Broker Datek Stakes 'Serious Turf' with $80 Mil," *Advertising Age,* 70 (October 18, 1999), 1-2.

22. Marvin E. Shaw and Philip R. Costanzo, *Theories of Social Psychology,* Second Edition (New York: McGraw-Hill, 1982), p. 334.

23. Kenneth E. Clow and Donald Baack, *Integrated Advertising, Promotion, and Marketing Communications* (Upper Saddle River, NJ: Prentice-Hall, 2002), p. 9.

24. Don Jeffrey, "Survey Details Consumer Shopping Trends on the Net," *Billboard,* 111 (May 29, 1999), 47-48.

25. Richard A. Shaffer, "Listen Up! Pay Attention! New Web Startups Want Ads That Grab You," *Fortune,* 140 (October 25, 1999), 348-349.

26. Olson and Reynolds, "Understanding Consumers' Cognitive Structures," Reynolds and Craddock, "The Application of the MECCAS Model."

27. David Aaker and Donald Norris, "Characteristics of TV Commercials Perceived As Informative," *Journal of Advertising Research,* 22 (1982), 61-70; Henry A. Laskey, Ellen Day, and Melvin R. Crask, "Typology of Main Message Strategies for Television Commercials," *Journal of Advertising,* 18 (1989), 36-41.

28. G. Douglas Olsen, "Observations: The Sounds of Silence: Functions and Use of Silence in Television Advertising," *Journal of Advertising Research,* 34 (September/October 1997), 89-95.

29. Michael Miller, "Even Out of Context, the Beat Goes On (and On)," *Pittsburgh Business Times,* 18 (November 27, 1998), 12.

30. David Tossman, "The Final Push—POP Boom," *New Zealand Marketing Magazine,* 18 (September 1999), 45-51.

31. Ibid.; Matthew Martinez and Mercedes M. Cardona, "Study Shows POP Gaining Ground As Medium," *Advertising Age,* 68 (November 24, 1997), 43.

32. The PACT Agencies, "PACT."

33. Don Jagoda, "The Seven Habits of Highly-Successful Promotions," *Incentive,* 173 (August 1999), 104-105.

34. www.Decisionanalyst.com; Patricia Riedman, "DiscoverWhy Tests TV Commercials Online," *Advertising Age,* 71 (March 27, 2000), 46-47.

35. Stephanie Thompson, "Big Deal," *MediaWeek,* 7 (November 24, 1997), 36; Judann Pollack, "Big G Has Special Cheerios for Big '00," *Advertising Age,* (June 14, 1999), 1-2.

36. Cyndee Miller, "Study Dispels '80s Stereotypes of Women," *Marketing News,* 29 (May 22, 1995), 3.

37. Geoffrey E. Meredith and Charles D. Schewe, "Marketing by Cohorts, Not Generations," *Marketing News,* 33 (February 1, 1999), 22.

38. David Gianatasio, "Smash's Sex Appeal," *Adweek—New England Edition,* 36 (September 13, 1999), 4.

39. Pat Sloan and Carol Krol, "Underwear Ads Caught in Bind Over Sex Appeal," *Advertising Age,* 67 (July 8, 1996), 27.

40. Jessica Severn and George E. Belch, "The Effects of Sexual and Non-Sexual Advertising Appeals and Information Level on Cognitive Processing and Communication Effectiveness," *Journal of Advertising,* 19 (1990), 14-22.

41. Ibid.

42. D.C. Bello, R.E. Pitts, and M.J. Etzel, "The Communication Effects of Controversial Sexual Content in Television Programs and Commercials," *Journal of Advertising,* 3 (1983), 32-43.

43. Michael L. Maynard, "Slice-of-Life: A Persuasive Mini Drama in Japanese Television Advertising," *Journal of Popular Culture,* 31 (Fall 1997), 131-142.

44. Ibid.

45. Alastair Goldfisher, "Firms Give Away Everything to Capture Trade-Show Traffic," *Pacific Business News,* 37 (April 2, 1999), 21.

46. David F. Polack, "Creativity Is Key to Successful Giveaway Marketing Campaigns," *Business Journal Serving Fresno and the Central San Joaquin Valley,* Issue 322532 (November 1, 1999), p. 4.

47. Sam Bradley, "Marketers Are Always Looking for Good Pitchers," *Brandweek,* 37 (February 26, 1996), 36-37.

48. Claire Murphy, "Stars Brought Down to Earth in TV Ads Research," *Marketing* (January 22, 1998), 1.

49. Cultural Sponsorship Can Help Reach the Affluent," *Bank Marketing,* 26 (October 1994), 7.

50. Herbert E. Krugman, "Why Three Exposures May Be Enough," *Journal of Advertising Research,* 12(6) (1972), 11-14.

51. Jack J. Kasulis, "Managing Trade Promotions in the Context of Market Power," *Journal of the Academy of Marketing Science,* 27 (Summer 1999), 320-332; Anthony Lucas, "In-Store Trade Promotions," *Journal of Consumer Marketing,* 13(2) (1996), 48-50.

52. H. Rao Unnava and Deepak Sirdeshmukh, "Reducing Competitive Ad Interference," *Journal of Marketing Research,* 31 (August 1994), 403-411.

53. Alf Nucifora, "Viral Marketing Spreads by 'Word of Net.'" *Business Journal (Central New York),* 14 (May 5, 2000), 25-26.

54. Laurie A. Babin and Alvin C. Burns, "Effects of Print Ad Pictures and Copy Containing Instructions to Imagine on Mental Imagery That Mediates Attitudes," *Journal of Advertising,* 26 (Fall 1997), 33-44.

55. Freddie Campos, "UH Facility Test Ads for $500," *Pacific Business News,* 35 (August 18, 1997), A-1-A-2).

56. Riedman, "DiscoverWhy Tests TV Commercials Online."

Index